Advances in Spatial and Network Economics

Martin J. Beckmann · Tönu Puu

Spatial Structures

With 40 Figures

Springer-Verlag Berlin Heidelberg New York
London Paris Tokyo Hong Kong

Professor Dr. Martin J. Beckmann
Technische Universität München, FRG
and Brown University, Providence, R.I., USA

Professor Dr. Tönu Puu
Department of Economics
Umeå University
S-90187, Umeå, Sweden

ISBN 3-540-51957-2 Springer-Verlag Berlin Heidelberg New York Tokyo
ISBN 0-387-51957-2 Springer-Verlag New York Berlin Heidelberg Tokyo

The use of registered names, trademarks, etc. in this publication does not imply, even in the absence of a specific statement, that such names are exempt from the relevant protective laws and regulations and therefore free for general use.

Printing: Weihert-Druck GmbH, Darmstadt
Bookbinding: J. Schäffer GmbH u. Co. KG., Grünstadt
2142/7130-543210

To the memory of our friend

Giorgio Leonardi

1942 - 1986

Preface

The common theme in the essays of this book is the emergence and survival of spatial structures. How are economic structures created in an otherwise homogeneous environment? The answer must be sought through an analysis of economic forces that operate in the two dimensional continuum of space. Ultimately these forces emanate from the fundamental fact that spatial concentration is needed to reap increasing returns to scale, i.e. to gather the fruits of the division of labour. Adam Smith's dictum: "The division of labour is limited by the size of the market" poses a fundamental question to spatial economic analysis: just how do markets operate when extended over distances?

Although these essays were written at different times they all relate to the problem of economic structures generated in spatial markets. They approach the phenomena of spatial order from different angles, but it is hoped in a connected and logically consistent way.

We thank the editors and publishers of the <u>Annals of Regional Science</u> for permission to reprint parts of the articles "On the Shape and Size of Market Areas" and "Population Growth and Dispersal" to be published this year. It is our pleasure to thank Mrs. I.Ströhlein for drawing several figures and Dr. H.Mittermeier for compiling the index. Last not least we are grateful to Mrs. B.Schwarzwälder for her patient job of typing and retyping this manuscript.

München May 9, 1989

Martin Beckmann   Tönu Puu

Table of Contents

1. The Genesis of Economic Centers: A Bifurcation Model

Fernand Braudel in "Civilization and Capitalism" (1979) designates the lowering of transportation costs as the prime motive force behind the development of the world economy. In his historical treatment of the matter transportation costs are of course very general, including such things as robbery by the medieval knights. Intuitively, it seems sound that specialization and spatial concentrations of population favour efficient mass production using increasing returns and division of labour. That this in turn depends on decreasing the impedance of communication is obvious. In this chapter we want to see how this works out with respect to increasing returns. Later we will return to this issue by taking a closer look at the concentration of population.

More precisely, we want to see how concentration of productive activities under increasing returns to scale occurs in the space economy when transportation costs are lowered. For this reason we assume a simple type of production function with increasing-decreasing returns to scale. To make the objective function simple we just look at the net output per capita over transportation costs, calculate the optimum radius of the market area, and compare the result with local production. We thus do not enter the question of who carries the costs of transportation nor the details of pricing policy. Transportation is assumed to be along straight lines, and the costs for it to be proportional to distance and volume transported.

1.1 One Dimension

The really interesting space economy is two-dimensional, but it is instructive to start with the simpler case of one dimension. Suppose we have a production function

$$Q = \alpha(\beta L^2 - L^3) \, , \tag{1}$$

where L denotes the input of labor. The constant α represents technological efficiency and β is twice the optimal scale of production in Frischian terminology (where marginal and average productivities are equal). See Frisch (1926). This power function is the simplest way of representing a technology of first increasing and eventually decreasing returns to scale, and is in fact the truncated Taylor series of any production function with these properties.

Suppose we have a market extended in one-dimensional space with a constant population density of 1/2. This value is chosen for the sake of convenience and does not affect any significant conclusions. If the radius of the market area is denoted R, then the population (=labour force) in this market area equals:

$$L = R .$$ (2)

Now suppose transportation costs are proportional to distance, measured in units of the output and denoted κ per unit of distance. Then total transportation costs for supplying the market area are:

$$T = \kappa R^2$$ (3)

The surplus of per capita output over transportation cost is:

$$\frac{Q - T}{L} = (\alpha\beta - \kappa)R - \alpha R^2 ,$$ (4)

and obviously it is maximal when:

$$R = \frac{1}{2}(\beta - \frac{\kappa}{\alpha}) .$$ (5)

Then maximum output over transportation costs is:

$$\left(\frac{Q - T}{L}\right)_{max} = \frac{\alpha}{4}(\beta - \frac{\kappa}{\alpha})^2$$ (6)

This yields the maximum proceeds from concentrated production using the increasing returns. This, however, has to be compared to the case of local production without wasting any resources in transportation. In this case local production per capita (remember there are now no transportation costs), calculated using the local population density of 1/2 as input, is:

$$\frac{q}{1} = \frac{\alpha(\beta(\frac{1}{2})^2 - (\frac{1}{2})^3)}{\frac{1}{2}} = \frac{\alpha}{4}(2\beta - 1) \ . \tag{7}$$

Local production is better whenever $q/1 > ((Q - T)/L)_{max}$, i.e. whenever:

$$(2\beta - 1) > (\beta - \frac{\kappa}{\alpha})^2 \ . \tag{8}$$

For high transportation costs local production is the better solution. From (5) we see that market radius decreases linearly with the ratio κ/α until (6) and (7) become equal. This is shown in Figure 1.1, where a family of such linear relations are drawn.

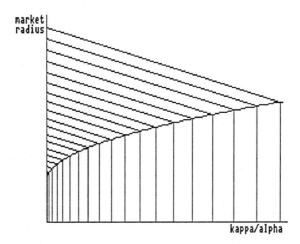

Fig.1.1 Dependence of market radius on transportation cost.

In the critical case where the inequality (8) holds as an equality, i.e. (6) and (7) break even, the straight lines end at a parabola. There is a bifurcation and the radius of the market area suddenly drops to zero. This means that the system bifurcates to local production only. The critical market radius can be easily calculated from (5) using the condition that (6) and (7) are equal. We find that the radius is:

$$R_{min} = \frac{1}{2} \sqrt{2\beta - 1} \quad , \tag{9}$$

Thus, whenever the scale parameter exceeds the threshold value 1/2, local production bifurcates to concentrated production with a finite market radius. This represents what is known as a hard bifurcation. Only in the boundary case with $\beta = \frac{1}{2}$ the bifurcation is soft. With smaller values of β no bifurcations occur. The constant 1/2 represents, as we recall, the density of population.

1.2 Two Dimensions: Circular Markets

In two dimensions shape becomes essential. In one-dimensional space there is only one shape: the interval. Its two-dimensional equivalent is the circular disc. As is well known circles cannot pave the plane without overlappings or interstices, so, we have to deal with hexagons, squares, and triangles, but the circles provide a convenient introductory case.

As in the one-dimensional case it is convenient to choose a suitable population density. With circular market areas we choose $1/\sqrt{\pi}$. Then we have the total population (=labour force):

$$L = R^2 , \tag{10}$$

in the market area, and incur the transportation cost:

$$T = \frac{2}{3}\kappa R^3 , \tag{11}$$

where κ again is the transportation cost rate.

The production function introduced above could in principle be kept, but it would lead to unnecessarily awkward expressions. So we prefer an equation with different powers of the terms, but with the same general properties as the original one:

$$Q = \alpha(\beta L^{1.5} - L^2) . \tag{12}$$

It is obvious that we can find a nonsingular coordinate transformation $x \rightarrow y$ that maps the function $f(x) = \alpha(\beta x^{1.5} - x^2)$ onto the function $g(y) = \alpha(\beta y^2 - y^3)$ on the interval $(0,\beta)$, preserving all the properties that interest us, i.e. the zeros, the maximum, and the inflection point.

The per capita excess production over transportation is slightly modified:

$$\frac{Q - T}{L} = (\alpha\beta - \frac{2}{3}\kappa)R - \alpha R^2 , \tag{13}$$

the radius at which it is maximal becomes:

$$R = \frac{1}{2}(\beta - \frac{2}{3}\frac{\kappa}{\alpha}) , \tag{14}$$

and its maximal value:

$$(\frac{Q - T}{L})_{max} = \frac{\alpha}{4}(\beta - \frac{2}{3}\frac{\kappa}{\alpha})^2 . \tag{15}$$

With the assumed population density the per capita output from local production is:

$$\frac{q}{l} = \frac{\alpha}{\pi^{1/4}} (\beta - \frac{1}{\pi^{1/4}}) . \tag{16}$$

The inequality telling when local production is more profitable now reads:

$$(\beta - \frac{1}{\pi^{1/4}}) > \frac{\pi^{1/4}}{4} (\beta - \frac{2}{3}\frac{\kappa}{\alpha})^2 , \tag{17}$$

and the critical radius to which the market areas bifurcate becomes:

$$R_{min} = \frac{1}{\pi^{1/4}} \sqrt{\pi^{1/4}\beta - 1} . \tag{18}$$

The hard type of bifurcation again occurs whenever $\beta > 1/\pi^{1/4}$. So, this case is in essence not different from the one-dimensional one.

1.3 Two Dimensions: Triangles, Squares, Hexagons

For the remaining cases: triangles, squares, and hexagons, there is no standardized population density that simplifies all the expressions, so let us just make it unitary. It is then as easy as anything to write general formulas for n-gons, covering all three cases and in the limit the circle as well.

For a regular polygon the area, and hence the quantity of labour to be substituted into the production function, is:

$$L = A_n R^2 , \tag{19}$$

where:

$$A_n = n \cos(\tfrac{\pi}{n}) \sin(\tfrac{\pi}{n}) . \tag{20}$$

Likewise, the transportation cost, being the integral:

$$\iint_{n-gon} \sqrt{x^2 + y^2} \; dxdy = \iint_{n-gon} r^2 dr d\theta$$

becomes:

$$T = \kappa B_n R^3 , \tag{21}$$

where:

$$B_n = \tfrac{n}{3}(\cos(\tfrac{\pi}{n})\sin(\tfrac{\pi}{n}) + \cos^3(\tfrac{\pi}{n})\ln(\tan(\tfrac{\pi}{4} + \tfrac{\pi}{2n}))) . \tag{22}$$

Substituting into the production function (12) we obtain for output per capita over transportation:

$$\frac{Q - T}{L} = (\alpha\beta \sqrt{A_n} - \kappa\frac{B_n}{A_n})R - \alpha A_n R^2 \ . \tag{23}$$

The optimum radius of the market area can then be determined as:

$$R = \frac{1}{2}(\frac{\beta}{\sqrt{A_n}} - \frac{\kappa}{\alpha} \frac{B_n}{A_n^2}) \ , \tag{24}$$

and the resulting maximum per capita output is:

$$(\frac{Q - T}{L})_{max} = \frac{\alpha}{4}(\beta - \frac{B_n}{A_n \sqrt{A_n}} \frac{\kappa}{\alpha})^2 \ . \tag{25}$$

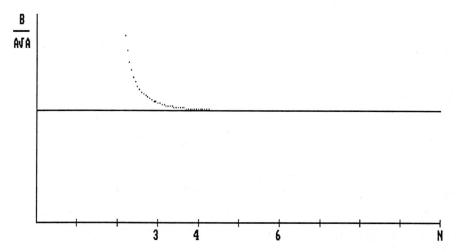

Fig. 1.2 Efficiency of triangles, squares, and hexagons as compared to the circle.

We can see from the expressions (20) and (22) that $B_n/(A_n \sqrt{A_n})$ decreases uniformly with increasing n, attaining a limit of $2/3\sqrt{\pi}$, reciprocal to the assumed population density. This is shown in Figure 1.2, where this dependence is depicted as a continuous curve, even though it makes no sense for nonintegral values less than three. The asymptotic value pertinent to the circle is shown as a horizontal line.

We conclude, not surprisingly, that, circles not being admitted, the hexagon is the best shape of the market area.

The bifurcation analysis can now be carried out exactly as before for each of the possible values 3,4, and 6 of n. Local production is superior to centralized provided that:

$$(\beta - \frac{1}{\pi^{1/4}}) > \frac{\pi^{1/4}}{4} (\beta - \frac{B_n}{\sqrt{A_n}})^2 . \tag{26}$$

It is thus also more likely that decreasing transportation costs make the system bifurcate to hexagonal than to square or triangular market areas, because there is an interval for the scale parameter where centralized production is superior for a hexagonal shape, but local production remains better for the other shapes. Of course it is even more likely that market areas first arise in the circular shape, provided technological progress (in terms of increasing returns at optimal operation scale, rather than of overall productivity) takes place at sufficiently distant points in space.

1.4 Conclusion

We conclude that when transportation costs are lowered the simple model presented here produces a hard bifurcation to a finite size of the market area from purely local production. The bifurcation is of a hard type, except for a boundary case, provided the production scale parameter exceeds a certain critical value. If the parameter is too low the system never bifurcates from the state of purely local production. We also see that the outcome does not depend on whether we assume a simple one-dimensional space, or deal with the real two-dimensional geographical space.

2. The Integrated State: von Thünen revisited

In the first chapter spatial concentration of production emerged as a result of increasing returns to scale. These prevail even in the face of increasing transportation costs incurred in the distribution of the product.

The spatial concentration of even one production activity gives rise to city formation. At the beginning stands the possibility of just one city and thus of the basic von Thünen Model:

Consider a very large town in the center of a fertile plain which does not contain any navigable rivers or canals. The soil of the plain is assumed to be of uniform fertility which allows cultivation everywhere. At a great distance the plain ends in an uncultivated wilderness, by which this state is absolutely cut off from the rest of the world.

This plain is assumed to contain no other cities but the central town and in this all manufacturing products must be produced; the city depends entirely on the surrounding country for its supply of agricultural products.

All mines and mineral deposits are assumed to be located right next to the central town.

The question now is: How under these circumstances will agriculture be developed and how will the distance from the city affect agricultural methods when these are chosen in the optimal manner?

It is customery to describe this allocation problem by means of a graph. In figure 2.1 the horizontal axis indicates distance from the city, and the vertical axis shows net revenue. For every agricultural product one may plot net revenue per ha, that is quantity produced per ha times price received at the city market minus costs of labor and material inputs, minus costs of transportation.

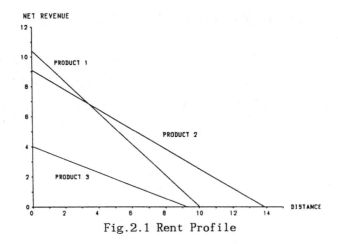

Fig.2.1 Rent Profile

This net revenue gives rise to a downward sloping straight line. Its intercept equals net revenue before transportation cost, and its slope the transportation cost of the output of one hectar over a unit distance. (Strict proportionality of transportation costs with respect to product quantity and distance is assumed).

When the net revenue of two products are compared two possibilities arise:

The net revenue curve of one product lies above that of the other product at all distances where net revenue is non-negative. Then the second product is dominated and would never be produced in this spatial market.

Or the curve of steeper slope intersects the other curve from above at some positive distance. In this case both products will be produced by profit maximizing land owners, each exclusively in that range of distances where its curve lies above the other.

This surprising result of complete specialisation in land use was first thought to be due to the assumption of fixed coefficients in agricultural production, that was made here implicitly. Actually it applies whenever the production functions involved show constant (or increasing) returns to scale.

With more than two products competing for land use it is always that
with the highest net revenue per hectar after transportation cost that
is selected. The order in which products appear as one moves away from
the center is that of decreasing weight produced per hectar (or at any
rate decreasing transportation cost for the output of one ha).
Eventually no product can bear transportation cost to market any more
and the land remains uncultivated or is left to subsistence farming
beyond the pale of the markets.

The basic principle, tacitly invoked by von Thünen, is the principle of
transversality, or structural stability. It is assumed that the conical
surfaces swept out by the net revenue lines rotating around an axis
fixed at the central city either do not intersect at all or if they do
intersect along circular boundaries separating the different cultivation rings. - Now there is a third possibility: the cones might coincide. In that case there would not be any specialization, as several
products are equally profitable to produce on areas of non-zero mea-
sure.

This possibility was obviously discarded by von Thünen as an unlikely
coincidence. In terms of modern mathematics the intersection of two
surfaces would have to be transverse. Formally, the dimensions of the
intersection curve (1) and at the surrounding space (3) should add up
to the same as the dimensions of the intersecting surfaces (2 + 2).
See Poston and Stewart (1978). Transversality is related to structural
stability as any slight change of the net revenue surfaces would change
a non-transverse intersection into a transverse one.

As already mentioned the original fixed coefficient production is of no
importance at all for the result. Moreover, as shown in Beckmann and
Puu (1985) the original simple straight line transportation systems
(associated with a not only isotropic but even constant transportation
cost) can be discarded in favour of any system of optimal (curved)
routes. The net revenue surfaces will then no longer be simple cones in
a geometrical sense, but topologically they are obtained from a regular
cone by a smooth coordinate change, and they still have the peaks at

the central city. The transversality principle, however, holds and is now less trivial. The outcome is still a system of (deformed) specialization rings.

The restrictions in the original von Thünen model can thus be removed one by one without affecting the result, thus demonstrating the insight shown in his choice of modelling principles. There still remains, however, one restrictive assumption: the prelocated central city, but even that can be dispensed with. The significance of the central city actually is that it is a location of maximum net revenue from the most profitable activity - i.e. of maximum land rent. (Likewise the significance of the von Thünen "wilderness" is that of zero land rent.)

If we deprive the "central cities" of this exclusive character it is not empirically unreasonable to retain local land rent maxima. We only need to dispense with the assumption that there is just one prelocated and unique land rent maximum. We can assume any number of land rent maxima in what would then be an "integrated" rather than "isolated" state, see Puu (1984). the land rent maxima would then be matched by local land rent minima (with not necessarily zero land rent), and so "wilderness" splits into located spots of lowest land rent.

In the appendix to this chapter we dwell extensively on the structural stability of transportation flow fields. It is seen that structural stability admits three types of possible singularities. In reference to the land rent surface (the surface patched together by dominant pieces of all the net revenue surfaces) they are maxima, minima, and saddle points.

Our interpretation is that the maxima correspond to "central cities", the minima to "wilderness". What about the saddle points? In terms of flow they are characterized by the fact that many optimal routes pass close by them but very few are incident. The saddle points thus are locations of particularly good transportation (far both from congestion and land scarcity in the cities, and from poor infrastructures in the wilderness), but without any economic significance.

In the development process they are natural candidates for locating new cities. Goods flow nearby - it is only necessary to give the location itself economic significance, making the flows incident, and transforming the saddles into maxima. This would, however, not upset the general structure, as the process would automatically create new minima and saddles around such new maxima. All that happens is that the mesh of the economic landscape becomes finer.

Around each maximum and minimum the specialization pattern is still ringshaped (topologically speaking as the zones are deformed in the general case). Around a saddle point it is sectoral instead.

2.1 Production

Assume a production and exchange economy, extended on a region of the two-dimensional Euclidean plane, where location coordinates are denoted by x and y.

There are n different productive activities, represented by the production functions

$$Q_i = F^i(K_i, L_i, M_i) .$$
(1)

Output of each commodity depends on the primary inputs of capital, K_i, labour, L_i, and land, M_i used in that production activity.

Assuming that the production functions are linearly homogeneous, we may divide through by the input of land, and obtain the areal density of output, $q_i = Q_i/M_i$, as a well-defined function,

$$q_i = f^i(k_i, l_i),$$
(2)

of the areal densities of capital and labour inputs, $k_i = K_i/M_i$, and $l_i = L_i/M_i$.

By the assumption of linear homogeneity, we have ruled out increasing returns. Moreover, by not including the location coordinates as explicit arguments in the production functions, we have assumed away all interregional productivity differences. Last, the aggregate stocks of capital and labour are assumed to be perfectly mobile. Considering a long-run equilibrium of production and trade, we even disregard relocation costs, so that capital rent and wages, in fact, become spatial invariants.

These assumptions may seem restrictive. However, there is a point in removing all the reasons employed in traditional economics to explain specialization and trade, as we are going to demonstrate that these phenomena occur in a natural way, even without comparative advantages, immobile inputs, or increasing returns. Introducing any of the traditional reasons for trade only reinforces the points we are about to make. To be quite precise, local uniform production without moving commodities around is a possibility where production opportunities are equal. The strength of von Thünen's principle lies in the fact that a complete pattern of specialization is determined whenever there is any inhomogeneity anywhere, even in the case of an accidental development from the uniform solution.

In essence the Ricardian and the neoclassical trade theories are both rejected as necessary explanations, and we reintroduce the von Thünen theory, where trade and specialization occur essentially because of the character of two-dimensional space itself.

The single immobile input we are considering is land itself, but its quality is assumed to be the same everywhere, and so its economic usefulness depends only on location. This usefulness will be reflected in a spatially variable land-rent. Later on we will find out that the variation of land rent becomes the clue to the whole structure of the space economy.

Suppose that a given production activity is established at a location, then the optimal capital and labour densities will be determined by the conditions that the marginal productivities of capital and labour, denoted f_k^i and f_l^i, equal the ratios of input to output prices. Thus

$$P_i f^i_k(k_i, l_i) = r,$$

$$P_i f^i_l(k_i, l_i) = w, \tag{3}$$

where p_i denotes the local price of the commodity, and r and w denote the rent of capital and the wage rate, respectively. Because of the assumption of costless relocation, r and w are, as already noted, spatial invariants. Accordingly, equations (3) and (4) determine k_i and l_i, and output q_i is then determinable everywhere from equation (2), once p_i is known. So is the rate of profit

$$\pi_i(p_i) = p_i f - rk_i - wl_i \tag{4}$$

from activity i.

Now, the total profits per unit of land, obtained by combining the various activities are

$$\sum_{i=1}^{n} \pi_i(p_i)m_i, \tag{5}$$

where m_i are the fractions of land used for the various activities. As $\pi_i(p_i)$ are independent of m_i, we note that expression (5) is linear in m_i. Assuming the total fraction of land disposable for production to be m, we get the linear constraint

$$\sum_{i=1}^{n} m_i = m. \tag{6}$$

The maximization of equation (5) subject to constraint (6) has an obvious solution: put $m_i = m$ for that activity for which π_i is maximal, and $m_i = 0$ for the other activities. If several of these π_i attain the same maximum value, then all these activities are equivalent, and m can be distributed in any way among them. Maximum profit per unit land area, obtained by putting each piece of land to the best possible use, obviously determines land rent, g. We denote it by

$$g = \max_i \pi_i \tag{7}$$

so that for any commodity actually produced

$$g = \pi_i(p_i) \ . \tag{8}$$

The condition for a mix of equivalent activities to occur is that (8) holds for all the activities actually established. In this context we should recall that the forms of the functions $\pi_i(p_i)$ are completely determined from technological factors as expressed by the production functions $f^i(k_i, l_i)$, and depend on nothing else.

Accordingly, equation (8) constrains the different commodity prices to vary over space in a very specific constellation that is determined by the production technologies.

2.2 Transportation

There is one important activity that has not yet been mentioned, namely the production of transportation services. For notational convenience, we assume these services to be produced by a technology of fixed input/output ratios. This assumption is not crucial, as any one of the activities listed in equations (1) and (2) would lead to the same conclusions as below.

Transportation of one unit of the commodities per unit of distance traversed requires the use of κ units of capital, λ units of labour, and μ units of land. for convenience of notation only, these input coefficients are not indexed. The substance of this is that we define the units of the commodities so that transportation costs are the same, which then implies that the input coefficients are the same.

As we are completely free to choose the units of measurement, we can, without restricting the generality of the analysis, define suitably small units of commodities that are heavy or bulky in comparison with those that are more easily transportable.

Local transportation cost is thus given by

$$h(g) = \kappa r + \lambda w + \mu g \, , \tag{9}$$

where land rent g is now the only spatial variable. Using the Beckmann (1952; 1953) continuous model of transportation, we interpret trade flows as vector fields, $\phi^i = [\phi_1^i(x,y)], \phi_2^i(x,y)]$. With each location we associate vectors whose norms $|\phi^i| = [(\phi_1^i)^2 + (\phi_2^i)^2]^{1/2}$ denote the volumes of traded commodities and whose directions, the unit direction fields, $\phi^i/|\phi^i| = (\cos\theta_i, \sin\theta_i)$ represent the actual directions of the flows of traded commodities. With this paradigm the conditions of optimum trade, provided it is taking place, are given by

$$h(g) \, \frac{\phi^i}{|\phi^i|} = \nabla p_i \, . \tag{10}$$

The spatial gradients of commodity prices are thus vectors which are codirectional with the flows of traded commodities, and they have norms equal to transportation costs. If there is no trade, the equalities are replaced by proper inequalities, so that the norms of the price gradients are less than the cost of transportation.

Condition (10) tells us two things. First, all interregionally traded commodities are shipped in the directions of their price gradients, that is, the directions of maximum price increases. Second, in these directions, prices increase at the rate of transportation costs. Concentrating on the second fact, we take norms of both sides of condition (10) and obtain

$$|\nabla p_i| = h(g) \, , \tag{11}$$

for all commodities actually transported.

2.3 Specialization and trade

The question is how equations (7) and (11) fit together. In connection
with equation (7) it was stressed that the prices of all commodities
actually produced would have to covary in a definite way over space.
This covariation was completely determined by the production technologies. Now, we see from equation (11) that another mode of covariation
is prescribed if the commodities are actually transported. As there is
only one degree of freedom (the land rent), we can expect difficulties
in fulfilling equations (7) and (11) for several commodities at once.
Formally, as g, according to equation (8) is a function of the single
variable p_i, we can easily get the absolute value of its gradient:

$$\pi_i' |\nabla p_i| = |\nabla g| \ . \tag{12}$$

where the prime denotes the derivative with respect to p_i. Accordingly,
for goods actually both produced and transported, the relations

$$\pi_i'(p_i) = \frac{|\nabla g|}{h(g)} \tag{13}$$

must hold identically over space.

We saw that π_i, and hence π_i', are independently determined by the production functions f^i. One such function, $\pi_i'(p_i)$, with $\pi_i^{-1}(g)$ substituted for p_i of equation (8), could be used to make equation (13) a
differential equation determining the function $g(x,y)$. But we could not
repeat the same trick with another commodity and hope that equation
(13) is reduced to an identity when g is already given.
At each location exactly one commodity is both transported and locally
produced. However, there may be any number of commodities only transported, or only produced for local consumption.

2.4 Land rent and spatial structure

We presently disregard production for local consumption, concentrating
on interregional trade. Still, as we are dealing with an arbitrary number of traded commodities, the picture might be incomprehensibly complex with all flows crossing each other. Observe that we have no a pri-
ori radial communication with a single "central city" as von Thünen
originally had. Accordingly, it might even be difficult to speak of any
structure of the space economiy.

However, the picture is very much simplified by some elementary obser-
vations. From equation (7) we conclude that, in any given specialization zone, the price gradient of the single actually produced and
transported commodity has the same direction as the land-rent gradient.
Thus, for this particular commodity, at least, the constant price lines
and the constant rent lines coincide everywhere in the zone, including
the boundaries. From the same equation we also see that the boundaries,
in fact, are lines of constant land-rent and hence constant price of
both the specialized commodities on either side of the boundaries.

This implies, however, that the boundary conditions are the same along
a common boundary for both commodity prices in the specialization zones
on either side of a common boundary. These prices are determined by the
same differential equation (11), and the only way their solu- tions
could differ would be by means of different boundary conditions. So,
except for space-invariant constants, the solutions for the prices
coincide, and the trajectories of trade issuing for a commodity in its
zone of specialization can be continued in the next zone, where they
are seen to coincide with the trajectories of trade issuing there, and
so on. Finally, all trajectory direction fields are seen to coincide.
In other words, all the price gradients are seen to coincide in direction with the land-rent gradient, not only in their proper zones of
specialization, but everywhere.

In the same way that the flow lines coincide for all commodities, so do
the contours of constant price. Thus, the constant price lines also co-

incide with the constant land-rent lines. As we have seen, some of the lines of constant land-rent become boundaries between adjacent zones of specialization.

The situation is now much simpler. To find out what the structure of the space economy looks like we need study only the variation of land rent in terms of the contours of constancy and the gradient lines. As a matter of fact, only the uniqueness makes it meaningful to speak of the structure at all. With the original picture of a possible mess of crossing direction-fields, this might not have been sensible.

2.5 The concept of structural stability

The structure, however, need not have such a simple character as in von Thünen's theory or in the "new urban economics", with the zones being concentric rings and the flows being radial to or from a unique centre. For all we know, the structure may take on so many different forms that it could be an impossible task to further describe or classify them.

In the following discussion we attempt a topological description of the structures, using only the principle that they should be robust to disturbances from factors not explicitly accounted for in the model. We will see that such a principle of resilience leads to a surprisingly precise topological description of the stable structures, which even rejects some rather basic ideas in spatial economics and economic geography.

We are going to make the concepts more precise. The trajectories traced by the land-rent gradient field can be defined by the pair of ordinary differential equations

$$\frac{dx}{ds} = \xi_1(x, y), \tag{14}$$

$$\frac{dy}{ds} = \xi_2(x, y), \tag{15}$$

where $\xi_1 = \partial g/\partial x$, and $\xi_2 = \partial g/\partial y$, by choosing a suitable parameter s.

Along with the system (14)-(15), consider another, slightly different system,

$$\frac{dx}{ds} = \eta_1(x, y) \ , \tag{16}$$

$$\frac{dy}{ds} = \eta_2(x, y) \ , \tag{17}$$

In the appendix we formalize how we conceive of the disturbances due to factors not explicitly accounted for in the model that we were discussing. Next, we need to set up a formal interpretation of the qualitative equivalence of the two sets of trajectories that solve the systems (14)-(15) and (16)-(17), respectively. If we can find a continuous one-to-one mapping (a homeomorphism) from the solution space of system (14)-(15) to the solution space of system (16)-(17), such that each trajectory is mapped onto a trajectory, and each singularity onto a singularity, the directions of trajectories and the types of singularities being preserved, then we certainly would regard the two solutions as qualitatively equivalent. If no such homeomorphism can be found, the solutions are not qualitatively, or topologically, equivalent. Intuitively, we would obtain the equivalence classes by imagining that the picture is drawn on a perfectly elastic rubber sheet. Then, all the pictures of land-rent gradients that can be obtained from such a picture by stretching without tearing are topologically, or qualitatively equivalent.

Now, the concept of structural stability is at hand. If the solution portrait of system (14)-(15) and the solution portrait of system (16)-(17) (the perturbed system) are qualitatively equivalent, then the system is structurally stable, if they are not equivalent, the system is unstable. In other words, if the perturbation only displaces and deforms the trajectories and singularities a little, but the directions and the types of each singularity are preserved, then we are dealing with structural stability. But, if trajectory directions are reversed, singularities appear, split, fuse, or disappear, then we are dealing with structural instability.

The question is: Why should we assume structural stability? The answer can be found in terms of strategy of scientific modeling. It is a good safeguard to use robust assumptions. As scientific modeling is always associated with abstraction from many facts of reality, one must take care that the conclusions do not crucially depend on some features in the assumptions that may not hold (see Arnold, 1983). For this reason we must admit perturbations. If such a strategy of prudent modeling helps us to fill the models with more specified information, the better it is.

The above idea of structural stability was formulated by Andronov and Pontryagin (1937). Later work by Morse, Smale, and Peixoto has provided the formal proofs of the general theorems in this field (see Peixoto, 1977). There are two remarkable theorems: the approximation theorem, and the characterization theorem.

The approximation theorem: In the abstract space of differential equations, those belonging to the subset of structurally stable ones form an open and dense set.

Hence, almost all possible differential equations are structurally stable, and each unstable system is in almost all directions completely surrounded by stable ones. This implies that we know more than that unstable systems would never persist in a world of change. We also know what the unstable systems are changed into if disturbed in almost every possible way.

To be exact, this only holds in two-dimensional space. Early hopes that these results could be extended to higher dimensions have been in vain, and in three-dimensions it is already possible to find unstable systems completely "surrounded" by other unstable systems. Fortunately, our obvious concern is two-dimensional geographical space. For explanation of the mathematics consult the works by Peixoto (1977) or by Hirsch and Smale (1974).

2.6 The topology of stable structures

Even more remarkable is the characterization theorem for structurally
stable systems. It tells us three things.

Characterization theorem
1 Almost everywhere the flow is laminar, that is, topologically
   equivalent to a set of parallel straight lines.
2 The exception is a finite set of hyperbolic singularities, that is,
   in our case of gradient-flow directions, nodes and saddles.
3 There is the global result that no trajectory incident to a saddle
   point at one end is incident to any saddle at the other.

The local characteristics already tell us something about the spatial
organization around singularities. A node, corresponding to a local
maximum of the land rent, is a point to which the trajectories of trade
in a neighbourhood converge as they do to the von Thünen central city.
The orthogonal trajectories of constant land-rent, among them the
boundaries of the specialization zones, more or less form concentric
rings. Around a saddle the spatial organization would seem to be secto-
rial. We will return later to an interpretation of this case.

What we want to do is more than that. We will see if it is possible,
using the characterization of stable systems, to draw a picture of a
regular tessellation or tiling of economic space as in the Christaller-
Lösch model. Of course, all we can aim at is a topological characterization, so that we have to admit all topological transformations by
stretching whatever picture we get in all possible ways.
As the flow is laminar, except at the singularities, we can use these
singularities (finite in number) as organizational elements, by arranging them in some regular pattern. As there are two main directions defined by the trajectories incident to the saddle points, it is natural
to arrange the points in a quadratic grid. As demonstrated in a previous work (Puu, 1979; 1982), it is easy to interpret such a square grid
as a basic graph of the stable flow. In figure 2.2 we start out from

any saddle point. Incident to it are one pair of ingoing and one pair of outgoing trajectories.

Because of the condition ruling out saddle connections, we know that these incident trajectories end up at nodes, one pair unstable, the other stable. As the stable and unstable nodes are arranged in opposite pairs, we note that there must be ingoing as well as outgoing trajectories to the singularities in diagonal directions from the original saddle point. But, the only admitted kind of singularity in our list, that has that property, is a saddle. Accordingly, we have found four new saddle points in the diagonal directions from the original one, and can continue the procedure, starting anew from each saddle, until every edge has been oriented and every singularity identified of the others of space. This is true if the numbers of different nodes are equal. We will see that triangular-hexagonal structures too are possible, provided the numbers of different nodes are in the specific ratio 2:1.

When we have oriented the basic graph of the stable flow, it is trivial to fill in any number of other trajectories, as in figure 2.3.
We can summarize our discussion of the regular structurally stable flow in the following theorem:
The land-rent surface itself is shown in figure 2.4 in the form of a "landscape" with hills, corresponding to the stable nodes, and valleys, corresponding to unstable nodes, euqally spaced in a lattice with saddles in the corners left between the hills and valleys.
Above we noted that the specialization pattern was defined by a set of constant land-rent contours. Thus, the orthogonal trajectories to the land-rent gradient lines in figures 2.2 and 2.3 becomes boundaries of the specialization zones. As already noted, the zones around any node have the shape of von Thünen rings.
To be more specific, we can interpret the stable nodes (local land-rent maxima) as the "central cities" of von Thünen and the unstable ones (land-rent minima) as "wilderness". As we are dealing, not with one "isolated state", but with a set of connected "states", it is natural that wilderness recedes to bounded areas, instead of completely sur-

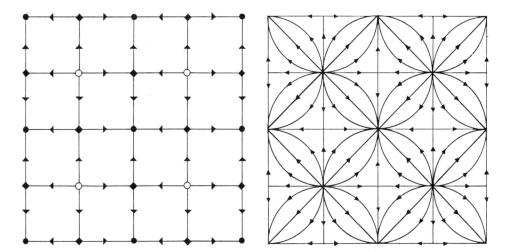

Figure 2.2 Basic graph of the
stable flow pattern.

Figure 2.3 Detailed flow portrait.

rounding the outermost ring. What we have done is to put a von Thünen
specialization pattern onto a subdivision of space between various central places with their "hinterlands", in the Christaller–Lösch spirit.
The Christaller–Lösch shapes may have to be dropped, as we have seen,
but the idea of subdivision of space with different centers remains.

We have interpreted the node singularities as the most central and the
most peripheral points in the system. It remains to give some interpretation to the saddle points. Their distinguishing feature is that trajectories of transportation seem to be attracted to them, so that they
must represent locations of particularly good transportation conditions. There seem to be two factors influencing those conditions. One
is competition for land, high land-rents, and possible congestion in
the central cities. The other is poor capacity of roads and sparse density of the network in the wilderness. Both are adverse to transportation. Accordingly, transportation is most favoured far from both types
of nodes. Such locations are the saddle points, and the tendency to
attract trajectories is accounted for.

In figure 2.5 is illustrated a specialization pattern corresponding to the flows depicted in figures 2.2 and 2.3. We can imagine that the black dots represent central business districts, surrounded by residential and industrial rings. the large discs can represent forests and the remaining connected area agriculture. The illustration and its interpretation are, of course, only examples.

The best picture would be obtained by superimposing the spatial organization from figure 2.5 onto the trade flow of figure 2.3, or, even better by drawing both superimposed pictures on the land-rent surface represented in figure 2.4. Such a picture would summarize our whole discussion.

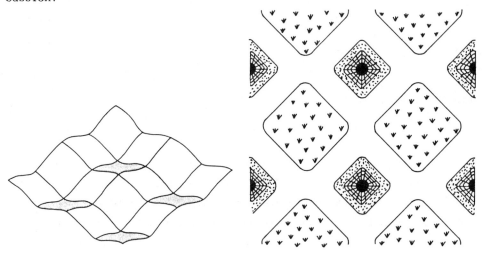

Figure 2.4 Land-rent surface.

Figure 2.5 Specialization pattern corresponding to flows in figures 2.2 and 2.3.

2.7 Concluding remarks

Using only general principles of production economics and the continuous model of trade, we have demonstrated that specialization and trade arise out of the character of bounded two-dimensional space and from general considerations of transversality. Accordingly, comparative advantages, immobile resources, and increasing returns were seen not to be necessary conditions for trade. In mainstream economics the general idea has been that specialization and trade are phenomena that need some specific conditions as explanation. We have seen that there are

much more general conditions explaining these phenomena; in fact, so
general that the absence of interregional trade, rather than its pres-
ence seems to need an explanation. This point, made by von Thünen 150
years ago, has been overlooked by trade theorists. This is not surprising, as economists have the habit of treating countries and continents
as points without spatial extension.

We were also able to establish a common direction-field for all the
flows of traded commodities. It was seen to be coincident with the direction field of the land-rent gradient. So, land rent, as determined
from the most profitable productive use to which it could be put, was
seen to determine the whole structure of the space economy.

Having thus established the meaningfulness of the structure concept in
a multi-commodity economy, we went on to characterize the structure
topologically. Using the concept of structural stability for the land-
rent gradient field, we were able to establish the basic stable organization of space.

Our picture of economic space was seen to resemble von Thünen's locally. But there were two differences. First, the characterization was topological, admitting all qualitatively equivalent transformations of
the basic picture. Second, we did not treat a single "isolated state",
but a number of such "state" connected in a chessboard pattern. Basically, we superimposed the von Thünen specialization zones around a
city onto a subdivision of space among central places and their
"hinterlands" along the lines of the ideas of Christaller and Lösch.
That their geometrical configurations could not be retained is another
story.

Appendix:

Structural stability as a modeling instrument in
spatial economics

A.1. Structural Stability

Arnold (1983) introduces the subject of structural stability in the
following words:

"In every mathematical investigation, the question
will arise whether we can apply our mathematical
results to the real world. Indeed, let us assume that
the result is very sensitive to the smallest change
in the model. In such a case, an arbitrarily small
change in the model (say a small change of the vector
field defining a differential equation) leads to
another model with essentially different properties.
A result like this cannot be transferred to the real
process under consideration, because, when
constructing the model, the real situation was
idealized and simplified ... Consequently the
question arises of choosing those properties of the
model of a process which are not very sensitive to
small changes in the model, and thus may be regarded
as properties of the real process".

Thus, structural stability of the models constructed is a question of
prudence in scientific research.

As an illustration Arnold takes the model of a pendulum. A model including friction is structurally stable, because a small change of the
friction coefficient only modifies the approach to equilibrium.
A model without friction, on the other hand, is structurally unstable,
as it represents an isolated case between damped and explosive motion,
and would be thrown into one of these classes by any change however
small it is. Arnold's point is that even if we knew nothing about friction in real life we should include it in order to produce a structurally stable model.

An economic analog is the case of classical multiplier-accelerator models of the business cycle, which in the linear version can produce
damped, explosive, or simple harmonic oscillations. If we wish to pro-
pose the model as an explanation of real business cycles, then we
should choose the damped variant. It might be tempting to choose the
case of simple harmonic motion, but we are advised by Arnold not to
believe that the parameters should be in that exact relationship which
produces the simple harmonic case. Even if we had estimated such a combination of parameters we should consider all the factors we have neglected by the abstraction process.

The illustration from business cycle theory also serves to make clear
the difference between structural stability and ordinary stability of
the ultimate equilibrium. The model for explosive oscillations, like
the one for damped oscillations, is structurally stable, even though
equilibrium is unstable in the explosive case and stable in the damped
case.
Structural stability, however, is like ordinary stability in another
respect. By assuming that the outcome of our modeling process is stable
- to displacements from equilibrium within the model context, or to
changes in the model structure itself - we gain information. There is
hence a reward for the prudent scientist who takes care not to produce
any unstable results, as he gains knowledge without access to any ex-
tensive factual information.

This is beautifully illustrated in the "correspondence principle" formulated by Samuelson (1947). Samuelson starts by complaining that "only
the smallest fraction of economic writings, theoretical and applied,
has been concerned with the derivation of operationally meaningful theorems". He defines such a theorem as "a hypothesis about empirical data
which could conceivably be refuted, if only under ideal conditions".
The problem seems to be general equilibrium economics where everything
depends on everything and anything is possible. Samuelson defines the
correspondance principle "between comparative statics and dynamics" so
that "definite operationally meaningful theorems can be derived". By
assuming stability in the dynamic model information is gained concern-

ing comparative statics. About assuming stability Samuelson writes:

"The plausibility of such a stability
hypothesis is suggested by the consideration that positions of unstable equilibrium, even if they exist, are tran-
sient, nonpersistent states, and hence
on the crudest probability calculation
would be observed less frequently than
stable states."

Above we saw that the flow lines could be found from the ordinary differential equations

$$dx/ds = \xi_1(x,y), \tag{18}$$

$$dy/ds = \xi_2(x,y), \tag{19}$$

where $\xi_1 = \partial g/\partial x$ and $\xi_2 = \partial g/\partial y$ and s is a suitably chosen parameter of the flow line x(s), y(s).

From the introductory quotation from Arnold the reader should have a good intuitive understanding of structural stability. To make the concept precise, however, we need some technicalities. Let it first be clear that we deal with a solution to equations (18) – (19), i.e. a "flow portrait" in two-dimensional euclidean space. To different pairs of differential equations we may expect that there are different flow portraits. Now, some of them only differ slightly from eachother with the trajectories and possible singularities displaced and deformed a little, but so that if the original picture is imagined as drawn on an elastic rubber sheet the new one can be imagined to be formed by stretching the sheet without tearing it.

This leads us to the concept of topological equivalence. Two flow portraits are topologically equivalent if we can find a coordinate transformation, say $x_1,y_1 \to x_2,y_2$, such that in the new coordinates each trajectory in the original flow portrait is mapped onto a trajec-

tory in the new one, and each singularity onto a singularity, directions and characters of singularities being preserved. The coordinate
transformation obviously has to be a homeomorphism, i.e. a continuous
map with nonvanishing Jacobian so that there is a continuous inverse as
well.

Next, we have to make precise what we mean by comparing pairs of differential equations that are only "slightly different". This will be
accomplished by defining an ϵ-perturbation of the system (18)-(19).
Suppose we deal with another set of differential equations:

$$dx/ds = \eta_1(x,y), \tag{20}$$

$$dy/ds = \eta_2(x,y) \tag{21}$$

such that

$$|\xi_i - \eta_i| < \epsilon , \tag{22}$$

$$|\partial \xi_i/\partial x - \partial \eta_i/\partial x| < \epsilon , |\partial \xi_i/\partial y - \partial \eta_i/\partial y| < \epsilon \qquad i = 1,2 \tag{23}$$

We say that (20)-(21) is an ϵ-perturbation of (18)-(19). The right hand
sides of the two pairs of differential equations differ by less than ϵ,
and the same holds for the partial derivatives. This pretty well catch-
es what we mean by the equations being slightly different. One might
just wonder by the little technicality of just including the first derivatives in the conditions. Concerning this the reader is referred to
the very clear explanation in Peixoto (1977) about why the derivatives
have to be included as otherwise the admitted class of deformations of
the differential equations would be so large that no structurally stable flow portraits corresponding to our intuitive understanding could
at all be found. Inclusion of higher derivatives, on the other hand,
would only make the definition unnecessarily narrow. The technicality
obviously has to do with the formulation of a flow pattern in terms of
a solution to a pair of differential equations.

We now combine the definitions of perturbation and topological equivalence. A flow portrait being a solution to differential equations of
the type (18)-(19) is said to be structurally stable if an ϵ-perturba-

tion of the system of equations produces a flow portrait that is topologically equivalent to the original one. Otherwise the system is
structurally unstable, when singularities split, fuse, or multiply or
if trajectories reverse direction by the slightest perturbation. Again,
we would not be interested in patterns that occasionally but very unlikely might occur, and so assume that the flow portrait produced by
(18)-(19) is structurally stable.

And now comes the reward for assuming structural stability. there is a
very rich Characterization Theorem for two-dimensional Flows. The reader is again referred to Peixoto (1977) or to the recent mathematical
set of "cartoons" on dynamics by Abraham and Shaw (1982-85). It is
shown that
  (1) the flow portrait is laminar, except at a finite number of
      singular points,
  (2) the singularities are "hyperbolic", in our case sinks, sources
      and saddles,
  (3) there is no connection between saddle points.
For a general system of differential equations spirals would be included in the set of admitted singularities, but in our case of gradient
dynamics they are excluded. The reason for this is simple as the gradient dynamics results from optimal choice of transportation routes where
it is never reasonable to circle around the destination an infinite
number of whirls before arriving.

A.2 Structurally stable tessellations

In view of the tradition in location and land use theory we would in
particular be interested in organizing tessellations of the plane in
regular polygons. From Kepler we know that there are only three regular
tessellations of the plane: the triangular, the square, and the hexagonal. In particular the hexagon has been cherished by scientists like
Christaller and Lösch. We only have to bear in mind that we are dealing
with topological properties; if a regular tessellation is structurally
stable any rubber sheet deformation of it is too. But this does not
matter as the tessellations are topologically different.

As the building blocks of regular tessellations are polygons: squares, triangles, and hexagons, they are all composed by triangular atomistic elements. We thus first have to identify this atomistic building block.

There are, as we have seen, two sets of curves representing spatial structure, the flow lines, and the orthogonal constant price contours. There are hence cells corresponding to the market areas in the monopolistic case centered around the source points, and cells corresponding to the central cities in the monopsonistic case centered around the sink points. The saddles naturally can be identified as the corners of the polygonal cells. However, dual to this set of cells there is another one, composed by trajectories of the flow and having all kinds of admitted singularities as vertices.

It does not matter which kind of cell structure we construct, the other follows automatically as a dual. As our considerations of structural stability have been applied to the flow it is natural to start with the skeleton of the flow made up by the singularities and the trajectories joining them. The unit cell in this skeleton can only be a triangle with one source, one sink, and one saddle point as vertices. This is easily seen by orienting the edges. We first note that there cannot be two saddles in the triangle as saddle connections were forbidden. Moreover, three nodes are impossible because then two nodes of the same type would have to be connected which would require opposite orientation of the same edge. The remaining possibility is two nodes and one saddle. The argument that nodes of the same kind cannot be consistently connected by a trajectory again serves to stipulate that the nodes be of different type. So, the remaining possibility is one saddle, one source, and one sink.

Our next task is to compose identical tessellation elements from these atomistic triangles. As shown in Puu and Weidlich (1986) we can accomplish this by arranging the atomistic triangles cyclically around, say, an unstable node. this is illustrated in Fig.2.6. For an equilateral triangle we need six, for a square eight, and for a hexagon twelve such atomistic triangles. Unlike the atomistic triangle itself, they can be used as tessellation elements so that the complete tessellation can be generated from one of these "molecules" by the use of rigid motion (translation and possibly rotation) only.

We, of course, have to convince ourselves that the choice of an unstable node did not crucially influence the result. Taking a stable node instead of the unstable one as the centre of the arrangement would interchange the roles of these two types of nodes. It is easy to see

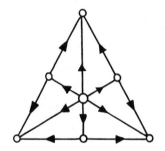 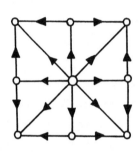 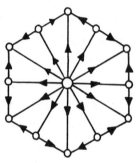

Fig.2.6 Tessellation elements.

that nothing at all is changed in the complete tessellations, except that, as we will see, the triangular-hexagonal polarity among sinks and sources is reversed.

Choosing a saddle point as centre, we first note that two atomistic triangles so arranged make up the sectors (three, four, and six respectively) from which equilateral triangle, square, and hexagon alike are composed. Hence, there is nothing new.

Four atomistic triangles cyclically arranged around a common saddle produce just a new sort of generator of the square tessellation.

Finally, six in the cycle produce a monkey saddle, illustrated in Fig.2.7, but this produces a new type of singularity, not admitted in structurally stable flows. There are six trajectories incident to the saddle and six hyperbolic sectors. Actually the saddle point does not admit more than four sectors, or it will lose its character. This is unlike the nodes, where we can combine any number of sectors due to the infinity of incident trajectories. We just reproduce the monkey saddle arrangement because it represents a transition case between the structurally stable tessellations. Although it can only have a passing momentary existence it is interesting as a transition case whose universality, as will be seen, has been established by Thom's catastrophe theory.

To close the argument we just note that the number of atomistic triangles in a cyclical arrangement must be even due to the necessity of a consistent orientation, and that it cannot exceed four. Hence, nothing new has been produced by choosing any other arrangement than that represented in Fig.2.6.

A quadratic arrangement was suggested by Puu (1979) by a different line of argument. The present discussion has closely followed that by Puu and Weidlich (1986), where the triangular and hexagonal arrangements were added to the list of stable possibilities. An important conclusion should, however be underlined. As in the triangle of Fig.2.6 three sinks are connected with the central source, and as six triangles would meet in each corner in the complete tessellation, we see that each source is connected to three sinks, whereas each sink is connected to six sources. Accordingly, the number of sources must be double that of sinks. We also note that in the case of a hexagonal tessellation the roles of sources and sinks is simply reversed, so that the number of sinks is double that of sources. In both cases, however the number of saddles equals the greatest number of nodes. In the case of squares we obviously have as many sinks as sources.

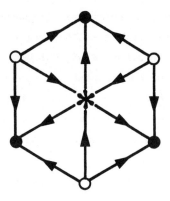

Fig.2.7 Monkey saddle.

By conclusion we note that in a structurally stable tessellation there have to be as many sinks as there are sources, or else, the arrangement may be triangular-hexagonal, but then the number of one sort of nodes has to be double that of the other. So far no new conclusions have been drawn. We will now turn to the transformations from one stable tessellation to another.

A.3. Transitions between stable tessellations

To study the transition between the different types of structure we can invoke Thom's catastrophe theory as already mentioned. As catastrophe theory only deals with gradient dynamics we again note how lucky we are. This fact, due, as we have seen, to optimization of transportation routes, not only excludes the occurrence of singularities of the spiral type but also enables a general study of structural transitions. We already suggested that the monkey saddle represents a transition case between the quadratic and hexagonal-triangular ones.

The monkey saddle occurs in the elliptic umblic catastrophe the canonical form of which is

$$\lambda = x_1^3 - 3x_1 x_2^2 .$$

(24)

See Poston and Stewart (1978) or Gilmore (1981). We have chosen the symbol λ for the potential, which earlier represented prices. As the flows indeed are derived from a gradient dynamics to the price potential this is no mere coincidence. the pattern of flows corresponding to this price potential according to (18)-(19) has to solve the differential equations:

$$dx_1/ds = 3(x_1^2 - x_2^2) ,\qquad(25)$$
$$dx_2/ds = -6x_1x_2 .\qquad(26)$$

It is easy to check that it fulfils the optimality conditions for transportation, provided we deal with a transportation cost function

$$k = 3r^2 ,\qquad(27)$$

where

$$r = \sqrt{(x_1^2 + x_2^2)} .\qquad(28)$$

However, this transportation cost function is the only one for which the monkey saddle flow is optimal. Any slight change in the cost function leads to a qualitatively different flow pattern, where the monkey saddle dissolves either in two dissociated ordinary saddles or in three saddles surrounding one source or sink. Actually all qualitatively different cases which can be produced from (24) are covered by these two cases as demonstrated in Thom's Classification Theorem.

Mathematically they can be obtained from the universal unfolding of (24) involving three parameters a, b, c and written

$$\mu = x_1^3 - 3x_1x_2^2 + \epsilon a(x_1^2 + x_2^2) + \epsilon(bx_1 + cx_2) .\qquad(29)$$

With a alone among the parameters different from zero any ϵ however small produces the split in three saddles and one node. With b, c different from zero instead the singularity splits in two dissociated saddles. Moreover, these are all phenomena that can occur whatever the actual perturbations are.

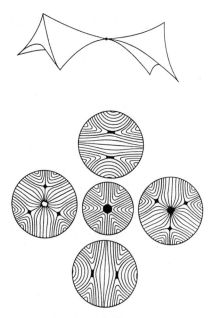

Fig.2.8 The elliptic umblic catastrophe. Bifurcation set in parameter
space (top) and flow portraits in coordinate space (bottom).

With a = 1 and b = c = 0 the corresponding transportation cost function
would have to be

$$k = (9r^4 + 4\epsilon^2 r^2 + 12\epsilon(x_1^3 - 3x_1 x_2^2))^{1/2} , \qquad (30)$$

where we use the definition (13) again. Likewise with a = 0 and
b = c = 1, we have

$$k = (9r^4 + \epsilon^2 + 3\epsilon(x_1^2 - x_2^2 - 2x_1 x_2))^{1/2} . \qquad (31)$$

It is easy to see that they reduce to (28) if ϵ is zero, as does (29),
although it is difficult to see how these changes of the transportation
cost function derived from the universal unfolding in canonical form
could be related to economic factors influencing transportation cost.
This, however, is always so. It is very difficult to work out the coordinate transformations that relate models of substance from positive
science to the general conclusions of catastrophe theory.

We just have to content ourselves with the fact that there is a general proof that those coordinate transformations exist so that we can be sure to have explored all possible phenomena, whatever the factors influencing transportation cost are and however they algebraically influence it.

It is now time that we tie the loose ends and really relate the elliptic umblic catastrophe to the transition of structure between quadratic and triangular-hexagonal patterns. To this end let us study Fig.2.8. The upper part depicts threedimensional a, b, c parameter space. The surface represents all the points where there is a transition of structure. Inside the surface we have the case of three saddles surrounding a node, outside it we deal with the case of two dissociated saddle points. The origin of parameter space only, where the surface

Fig.2.9 Monkey saddle tessellation.

shrinks together to a point, represents the monkey saddle case. In the lower part of the figure the flow patterns in coordinate space are illustrated in relative positions hinting at the directions in parameter space.

In Fig.2.9 we illustrate the case of a tessellation composed by nodes and monkey saddles, essentially hexagonal in character. We note that there are as many sinks as there are sources. Let us just recall that

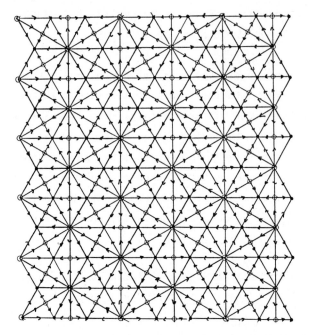

Fig.2.10 a) Triangular–Hexagonal Tessellation.

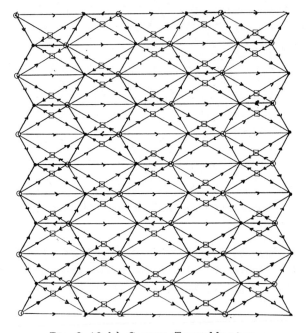

Fig.2.10 b) Square Tessellation

we deal with a case corresponding to the central picture in the flow portrait medaillons in Fig.2.8. Obviously the case is possible provided that transportation cost is exactly equal to the square of the distance from the closest monkey saddle, according to (27) and that this holds in a neighbourhood of each monkey saddle.

Remember, however that the situation depicted is utterly unstable, and that almost any disturbance of the transportation cost function will split the monkey saddles into either a pair of dissociated saddle points, or into a triplet of saddles surrounding a node. In the first case the number of sinks and sources is left unchanged, in the second either is doubled. These changed tessellations are illustrated in Fig.2.10.

Below we find the case where each monkey saddle splits into two dissociated saddles. It is not difficult to see that the resulting pattern is essentially square and could easily be brought into that shape by a suitable coordinate transformation. Above we find the other possibility where new sinks have been created and where we deal with a hexagonaltriangular tessellation of the stable type.

We have seen how the structurally stable tessellation can be transformed into eachother by small perturbations of the transportation cost function.

3. The Shape and Size of Löschian Market Areas[1]

3.1. Introduction

In this chapter we return to the perfectly homogeneous plain settled by
a population at a uniform density. Let a consumption good be produced
in economic centers rather than in all locations for the reasons dis-
cussed in chapter 1. The problem to be studied in this chapter concerns
to spacing -or density- of such centers and the shape of their market
areas. Two questions arise: what spacing is optimal and what spacing
results under free entry into a spatial market with specified conditions of competition?

Regarding the first question, it was Lösch who has said: "The real duty
of the economist is not to explain this miserable reality, but to im-
prove it" (p.4).

Lösch's analysis of the two problems suggests that in his view free entry creates a long run equilibrium that is optimal, at least optimal in
the sense of "maximizing the number of independent enterprises"(p.109).
He concluded that the shapes of market areas must be hexagonal and that
this would permit minimal distances between adjustant forms.

It came as quite a shock to the Löschians when Mills and Lav in 1964
showed that it is possible to have a long run equilibrium under free
entry in which the shape of markets is not hexagonal. They conjectured
octagonal markets as the outcome in these cases. I showed subsequently
that the shape must be one of a rounded hexagons or hexagonally flat-
tened circle. (Beckmann 1971).

---

[1]This chapter is based on the article "On the Shape and Size of Market
Areas" by Martin J. Beckmann, the Annals of Regional Science (1989).

In a recent paper Masao Toshiharu and Toda Ishikawa on "The Shapes of
Market Areas and Welfare" have reopened the question of the shape of
market areas. They consider a welfare optimum rather than a free entry
market equilibrium. Unfortunately their comparison is limited to the
three regular tesselations and do not include the possibility of rounded hexagons.

Now the whole question about the exact shape of market areas under either free entry or a welfare maximum reeks somewhat of the "fallacy of
misplaced concreteness" There is not more than a 17.3% difference between the area of a circle and its incribed hexagon. We do not expect
to identify rounded hexagons in the real world. Where it could make a
difference, however, is in planning. It is said that the Dutch did locate villages in the reclaimed land from the Zuider Zee in accordance
with Löschian precepts. Rounded hexagons would then result in some corner areas that are not reached by some producers and distributors of
village products and hence should not be settled. They would be in the
nature of forest or wilderness preserves. The recreational potential of
these left out corners should, however, be brought into the welfare
function explicitly. But in principle, it can make a difference what
the exact shape of optimal market areas turns out to be.

3.2. Simplified Analysis

Before engaging in a formal analysis it is always a good idea to try
one's intuition. Consider first an extreme case where the fixed cost is
so high that firms can just barely survive if allowed to charge monopoly prices under free entry. Bare survival requires circular market areas. When fixed costs are lower by an epsilon, then a welfare maximum
would clearly call for the existence of such an industry and for (almost) circular market areas.
At the other extreme we have very low fixed costs and hence many firms
with small market radii. Let 2R be the optimal distance between neigh-
bouring firms. A potential market area is then cut out for each firm by
its six immediate neighbours. It has the shape of a hexagon. In fig.3.1
we show a triangle representing 1/12 of this hexagon.

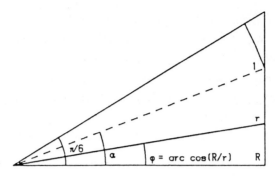

Figure 3.1 Representative triangle

Now let R be so small that marginal production cost plus transportation cost to any point in this hexagon is below the intercept of the demand function. Then every point is served in this market that makes a positive contribution to the producers' and consumers' surplus. Therefore the entire potential market area should be served. The optimal market area is the entire hexagon.

We canot escape the conclusion that there must be other possibilities between these two extremes.

Suppose in fact that there is a distance below the value of the maximal distance in the triangle of $\dfrac{2}{\sqrt{3}}$ R at which the price, i.e. the sum of marginal production cost plus transportation cost becomes equal to the demand intercept. Then delivery should stop at that critical distance. The result is that the hexagon is not filled out any more but the market boundary is partly a circle, partly the flat side of the limiting hexagon. This is the qualitative result of the analysis to follow.

3.3. Formal Analysis

For a rigorous analysis we make the following conventional assumptions.
- A homogeneous plain of uniform fertility settled by an agricultural population at a uniform density conveniently set equal to unity.
- A single industrial product produced by firms whose cost functions are identical consisting of a fixed cost F and a proportional cost c. (The latter can be disregarded and conveniently set equal to zero).

- Identical linear demand functions

  $q = 1 - p$ where   (1)

  q = quantity

  p = price paid by the consumer.

- Transportation cost proportional to distance and quantity of the product, standardized at unity.

- Euclidian distance r to be used in calculating transportation cost.

These assumptions while convenient seem unnecessarily restrictive; the qualitative results are in fact valid under much more general conditions.

- Welfare is defined as the sum of consumers plus producers surplus. A price $p + r$ at distance r generates a quantity demanded of

  $1 - p - r$,

  and a consumers surplus of

  $\frac{1}{2}(1 - p - r)^2$

  and a producers surplus (profit) of

  $p(1 - p - r)$

The aggregate consumers plus producers surplus is then

$$\int [\frac{1}{2}(1 - p - r)^2 + p(1 - p - r)] \, \rho(r) dr - F \qquad (2)$$

where $\rho(r)$ is the density of consumers served at a distance r in the market area under consideration. For a circular market $\rho(r) = 2\pi r$.

It is easily seen that the welfare maximizing mill price p equals marginal production cost, here assumed to be zero. We shall consider this suitably simple case.

Then the maximal distance to which deliveries are made is unity. The integral (4) becomes

$$12 \int\limits_{0}^{\frac{\pi}{6}} \int\limits_{0}^{Min[\frac{R}{\cos \varphi}, 1]} \tfrac{1}{2}(1 - r)^2 \; r \; dr \; d\varphi - F$$

$$= 12 \cdot (\tfrac{\pi}{6} - \alpha) \cdot \int\limits_{0}^{1} \tfrac{1}{2}(1 - r)^2 \; r \; dr + 12 \int\limits_{0}^{\alpha} \int\limits_{0}^{\frac{R}{\cos \varphi}} \tfrac{1}{2}(1 - r)^2 \; r \; dr \; d\varphi - F \qquad (3)$$

where

$$\cos \alpha = R \qquad \text{and} \qquad 0 \le \alpha \le \tfrac{\pi}{6} . \qquad (4)$$

(cf fig. 3.1).

The object is to maximize welfare per unit area. The welfare integral (3) must be divided by the area of the hexagon that represents the potential market area. It equals

$$A = 12 \cdot \tfrac{1}{2} R \cdot R \tan \tfrac{\pi}{6}$$

$$A = 2 \cdot \sqrt{3} \cdot R^2 \qquad (5)$$

Omitting the factor $\dfrac{6}{2\sqrt{3}}$ the maximand becomes

$$\frac{\int\limits_{0}^{\frac{\pi}{6}} \int\limits_{0}^{Min[\frac{R}{\cos \varphi}, 1]} (1 - r)^2 \; r \; dr \; d\varphi - F/6}{R^2} \qquad (6)$$

We consider first the case of a pure hexagon. This arises when $\dfrac{R}{\cos \varphi} \le 1$ for all φ in $0 \le \varphi \le \tfrac{\pi}{6}$, i.e. when

$$R \le \cos \tfrac{\pi}{6} = \frac{\sqrt{3}}{2} .$$

It is achieved when F is sufficiently small (see below), say

$$F \leq F_o$$

The maximand becomes

$$\underset{R}{\text{Max}} \quad \frac{1}{R^2} \int_0^{\frac{\pi}{6}} \int_0^{\frac{R}{\cos \varphi}} (r - 2r^2 + r^3) dr \, d\varphi - \frac{F}{6R^2}$$

$$= \underset{R}{\text{Max}} \int_0^{\frac{\pi}{6}} \left(\frac{1}{2} \frac{1}{\cos^2 \varphi} - \frac{2}{3} \frac{R}{\cos^3 \varphi} + \frac{R^2}{4\cos^4 \varphi} \right) d\varphi - \frac{F}{6R^2}$$

Differentiating with respect to R and setting this zero yields

$$0 = \frac{F}{3R^3} - \frac{2R}{3} \int_0^{\frac{\pi}{6}} \frac{d\varphi}{\cos^3 \varphi} + \frac{R}{2} \int_0^{\frac{\pi}{6}} \frac{d\varphi}{\cos^4 \varphi}$$

or

$$F = R^3 \cdot 2 \int_0^{\frac{\pi}{6}} \frac{d\varphi}{\cos^3 \varphi} - R^4 \frac{3}{2} \int_0^{\frac{\pi}{6}} \frac{d\varphi}{\cos^4 \varphi}$$

$$F = \left[\frac{\sin \frac{\pi}{6}}{\cos^2 \frac{\pi}{6}} + \ln \, \text{tg}(\frac{\pi}{4} + \frac{\pi}{12}) \right] R^3 - \left[\frac{1}{2} \frac{\sin \frac{\pi}{6}}{\cos^3 \frac{\pi}{6}} + \text{tg} \, \frac{\pi}{6} \right] R^4$$

Finally

$$F = \left(\frac{2}{3} + \frac{1}{2} \ln 3 \right) R^3 - \frac{5}{3\sqrt{3}} R^4$$

$$ \hspace{10cm} (7)$$

$$F = 1.216 \, R^3 - .962 \, R^4$$

The second order condition for a maximum requires that the horizontal line F be intersected with the rising branch of the polynomial (7) to obtain the R value that maximizes welfare per area. This polynomial is shown in figure 3.2 It turns out that the right hand side of (7) is rising throughout the range

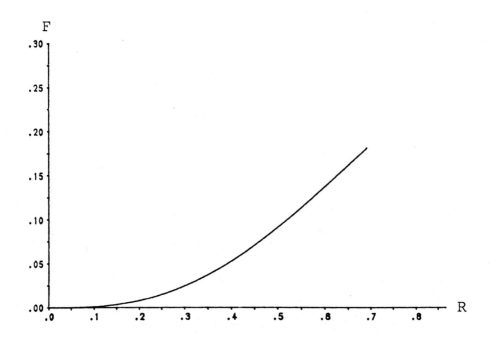

Fig.3.2 $F = 1.216 \, R^3 - 0.962 \, R^4$

$0 \leq R \leq \dfrac{\sqrt{3}}{2}$. The largest hexagon is obtained when $R = \cos \dfrac{\pi}{6} = \dfrac{\sqrt{3}}{2}$. The associated value of the fixed cost F is

$$F_0 = (\tfrac{2}{3} + \tfrac{1}{2} \ln 3) \, \frac{3\sqrt{3}}{8} - \frac{5}{3\sqrt{3}} \cdot \frac{9}{16}$$

$$= \frac{\sqrt{3}}{16} \cdot (3 \ln 3 - 1)$$

$$F_o = .2485316 \tag{8}$$

3.4. The Scope for Rounded Hexagons

When $F > F_o$ we enter the realm of rounded hexagons. From fig.3.1

$$R = \cos \alpha. \tag{4}$$

The integral (3) becomes

$$(2\pi - 12\alpha) \int_0^1 \frac{1}{2}(1 - r)^2 \, r \, dr + 12 \int_0^{\alpha} \int_0^{\frac{\cos\alpha}{\cos\varphi}} \frac{1}{2}(1 - r)^2 \, r \, dr \, d\varphi - F$$

Welfare per area is then proportional to

$$\frac{(2\pi - 2\alpha) \cdot \frac{1}{24} - F}{\cos^2\alpha} + 12 \int_0^{\alpha} \frac{1}{4} \frac{1}{\cos^2\varphi} - \frac{1}{3} \frac{\cos\alpha}{\cos^3} + \frac{1}{8} \frac{\cos^2\alpha}{\cos^4\varphi} \, d\varphi \tag{9}$$

Differentiating with respect to α and setting this zero yields

$$0 = - \frac{1}{24} \cos^2\alpha + 2 \cos\alpha \sin\alpha \, [\frac{1}{24} \cdot (\frac{\pi}{6} - \alpha) - \frac{F}{12}]$$

$$+ \frac{1}{24} \frac{1}{\cos^2\alpha} + \frac{\sin\alpha}{3} \int_0^{\alpha} \frac{d\varphi}{\cos^3\varphi} - \frac{2 \cos\alpha \sin\alpha}{8} \int_0^{\alpha} \frac{d\varphi}{\cos^4\varphi}$$

or

$$F = \frac{\pi}{12} - \frac{\alpha}{2} \, 2 \cos^3\alpha \int_0^{\alpha} \frac{d\varphi}{\cos^3\varphi} - \frac{3}{2} \cos^4\alpha \int_0^{\alpha} \frac{d\varphi}{\cos^4\varphi}$$

$$- \frac{\pi}{12} - \frac{\alpha}{2} + \cos^3\alpha \cdot [\frac{\sin\alpha}{\cos^2\alpha} + \ln \, \text{tg}(\frac{\pi}{4} + \frac{\alpha}{2}) - \frac{\cos^4\alpha}{2} [\frac{\sin\alpha}{\cos^3\alpha} + 2 \, \text{tg} \, \alpha]$$

$$F = \frac{\pi}{12} - \frac{\alpha}{2} + \frac{1}{2} \sin\alpha \cos\alpha - \sin\alpha \cos^3\alpha + \cos^3\alpha \cdot \ln \, \text{tg}(\frac{\pi}{4} + \frac{\alpha}{2}) \tag{10}$$

Equation (9) determines the angle α and hence $R = \cos \alpha$ as a function of F.

For $\alpha = \frac{\pi}{6}$ we obtain once more the expression (8) for F_o. When $\alpha = 0$ the market area becomes a circle and F takes on its maximal value

$$F_1 = \frac{\pi}{12} = 0.2617994$$

Rounded hexagons occur therefore in the region

$$F_o = 0.2485 \leq F \leq 0.2618 = F_1$$

This is but 5% of the full range of fixed costs from zero to $\frac{\pi}{12}$ that admit a welfare generating industry.

Figure 3.3 shows R as a function of F in the full range

$$0 \leq F \leq \frac{\pi}{6}$$

or

$$0 \leq R \leq 1.$$

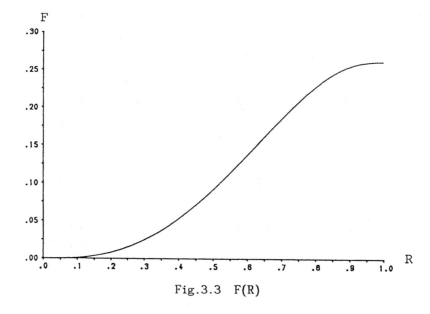

Fig.3.3   F(R)

3.5. Market Equilibrium with Free Entry

Turn now to the shape and size of market areas under Löschian monopoly and free entry. Using a profit maximizing mill price of

$$p = \frac{1}{2}(1 - \bar{r}) \tag{11}$$

(cf. Beckmann 1975, p.621)
the firm achieves profits of

$$G = \frac{1}{4} A \cdot (1 - \bar{r})^2 \tag{12}$$

where

$$A = \int_0^R \rho \ dr$$

is the total number of consumers served and

$$\bar{r} = \frac{\int_0^R r \ \rho(r)dr}{\int_0^R \rho \ dr} \tag{13}$$

is the average distance to customers in a market of given radius R.

Consider only the case of hexagonal market areas. To apply these results one finds from figure 3.1 that a spacing of firms at distances 2R
generates a market radius of

$$r = \frac{R}{\cos \frac{\pi}{6}} = \frac{2R}{\sqrt{3}} \tag{14}$$

The area of a hexagon of radius r is

$$A(r) = (2 \cdot \frac{1}{2} \cdot r \cos \frac{\pi}{6} \cdot r \sin \frac{\pi}{6}$$

$$A(r) = \frac{3\sqrt{3}}{2} r^2 = 2.598 \ r^2 \tag{15}$$

The average distance is, observing figure 3.1,

$$\bar{r}(r) = \frac{12}{A(r)} \cdot \int_0^{\frac{\pi}{6}} \int_0^{\frac{r \cos \frac{\pi}{6}}{\cos \varphi}} r^2 \ dr \ d\varphi$$

$$= \frac{12 \cdot \frac{1}{3} \cdot \cos^3 \frac{\pi}{6} \int_0^{\frac{\pi}{6}} \frac{r^3}{\cos^3 \varphi} \ d\varphi}{\frac{3}{2} \sqrt{3} \ r^2}$$

$$= \frac{1}{2} \ [\frac{\sin \frac{\pi}{6}}{\cos^2 \frac{\pi}{6}} + \ln \ tg(\frac{\pi}{4} + \frac{\pi}{12})]r$$

$$\bar{r} = (\frac{1}{3} + \frac{1}{4} \ln 3) \cdot r = 0.6079864 \ r \tag{16}$$

Application to $r = \frac{2}{\sqrt{3}} R$ yields

$$\bar{r}(R) = (\frac{1}{3} + \frac{1}{4} \ln 3) \cdot \frac{2}{\sqrt{3}} R = (\frac{2}{3\sqrt{3}} + \frac{1}{2\sqrt{3}} \ln 3)R$$

$$\bar{r} = .7020422 \ R$$

Profits considered as a function of R are therefore

$$G(R) = \frac{1}{4} \cdot \frac{3\sqrt{3}}{2} (\frac{2R}{\sqrt{3}})^2 \cdot (1 - 0.7020422 \ R)^2 - F$$

$$= \frac{\sqrt{3}}{2} R^2 (1 - 0.702 \ R)^2 - F$$

In equilibrium and free entry this must be zero.

$$F = 0.8660254\ R^2\ (1 - 0.7020422\ R)^2 \tag{17}$$

The graph of this function is shown in figure 3.4.

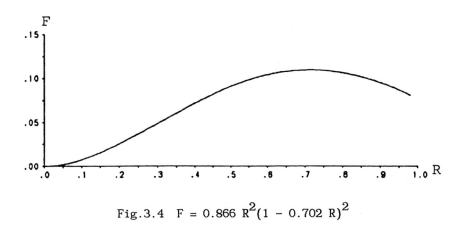

Fig.3.4 $F = 0.866\ R^2(1 - 0.702\ R)^2$

3.6. Comparison

Our main objective is to compare the size or radius of market areas in Löschian equilibrium with those of a welfare optimum. We shall limit ourselves to that range of fixed costs that result in hexagonal market areas. Denote the right hand side of (17) by ϕ_L (R) and the right hand side of (7) by ϕ_w.

Using abbreviations for the coefficients write

$$\phi_L \equiv b \cdot R^2 \cdot (1 - \mu R)^2 \tag{18}$$

$$\phi_w \equiv a_3\ R^3 - a_4\ R^4 \tag{19}$$

Now

$$\phi_L - \phi_w = bR^2 - 2b\mu R^3 + b\mu^2 R^4 - a_3 R^3 + a_4 R^4$$

$$\frac{\phi_L - \phi_w}{R^2} = b - (2b\mu + a_3)R + (b\mu + a_4)R^2$$

A straight forward calculation shows that

$$\frac{\phi_L - \phi_w}{R^2} \sim (R - .7238)^2 - .1323 \tag{20}$$

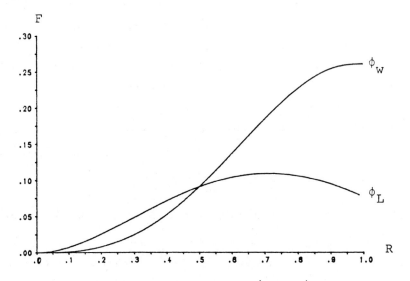

Figure 3.5 Comparison of ϕ_w and ϕ_L

It follows that

$$\phi_L - \phi_w > 0$$

whenever

$$|\, 0.7238 - R \,| > \sqrt{.1323} = .3637$$

or

$$R < .7238 - .3637 = .3601 \tag{21}$$

This corresponds to a bound for F

$$F < .0966 \; R^2 \; (1 - 0.702 \; R)^2 = 0.0626 \tag{22}$$

We conclude, free entry generates more firms than welfare optimization whenever R < .36, i.e. F < .0626. For all larger fixed costs F in the admissable range (for hexagons) of

$$F \leq .2485316$$

there are too few rather than too many firms in Löschian equilibrium. Economic theory based on spaceless analysis is wrong and intuition based on casual empiricism is right in suspecting that the density of firms is too small in free spatial markets, except for those industries that support a large number of firms to begin with. Then their density is too large. (Fig.3.5)

3.7. Choosing among Tesselations

We conclude by comparing welfare under various tesselations and show that among them the hexagon is best.

The area of a regular n-polyhedron with inscribed circle of radius R is

$$A = 2n \cdot \frac{1}{2} \cdot R \cdot R \text{ tg } \frac{\pi}{n} = n R^2 \text{ tg } \frac{\pi}{n}$$

Welfare is

$$W = 2n \int_0^{\frac{\pi}{n}} \int_0^{\frac{R}{m_\varphi}} \frac{1}{2}(1 - r)^2 r \, dr \, d\varphi - F$$

$$W = n \int_0^{\frac{\pi}{n}} \frac{R^2}{2m^2_\varphi} - \frac{2}{3} \frac{R^3}{m^3_\varphi} + \frac{1}{4} \frac{R^4}{m^4_\varphi} \, d\varphi - F \tag{1}$$

Welfare per area - which is assumed to fill out the entire plane (thus limiting n to 3,4,6) is then

$$\frac{W}{A} = \frac{1}{tg\,\frac{\pi}{n}} \int_o^{\frac{\pi}{n}} \frac{1}{2m^2\varphi} - \frac{2}{3}\frac{R}{m^3\varphi} + \frac{R^2}{4}\frac{1}{m^4\varphi}\,d\varphi - \frac{F}{nR^2 tg\,\frac{\pi}{n}}$$

Maximizing welfare per unit areas yields

$$0 = \frac{2F}{nR^3 tg\,\frac{\pi}{n}} - \frac{1}{tg\,\frac{\pi}{n}} \cdot [-\frac{2}{3}\int_o^{\frac{\pi}{n}}\frac{d\varphi}{m^3\varphi} + \frac{R}{2}\int_o^{\frac{\pi}{n}}\frac{d\varphi}{m^4\varphi}]$$

$$\frac{F}{n} = \frac{R^3}{3}\int_o^{\frac{\pi}{n}}\frac{d\varphi}{m^3\varphi} - \frac{R^4}{4}\int_o^{\frac{\pi}{n}}\frac{d\varphi}{m^4\varphi} \tag{2}$$

$$\frac{F}{n} = \frac{R^3}{6} \cdot [\frac{\sin\frac{\pi}{n}}{\cos^2\frac{\pi}{n}} + \ln\tan\,(\frac{\pi}{4} + \frac{\pi}{2n})]$$

$$- \frac{R^4}{12}[\frac{\sin\frac{\pi}{n}}{\cos^3\frac{\pi}{n}} + 2\tan\frac{\pi}{n}]$$

For n = 4 this yields

$$F = R^3 \cdot \frac{2}{3}[\frac{\sin\frac{\pi}{4}}{\cos^2\frac{\pi}{4}} + \ln\tan\,(\frac{3\pi}{8})]$$

$$- R^4 \cdot \frac{1}{3}[\frac{\sin\frac{\pi}{4}}{\cos^2\frac{\pi}{4}} + 2\tan\frac{\pi}{4}]$$

$$= R^3 \cdot \frac{2}{3}[\frac{\frac{1}{\sqrt{2}}}{(\frac{1}{\sqrt{2}})^2} + \ln\tan\frac{3\pi}{8}]$$

$$- R^4 \frac{1}{3} \left[\frac{\frac{1}{\sqrt{2}}}{(\frac{1}{\sqrt{2}})^3} + 2 \cdot 1 \right]$$

$$= R^3 \frac{2}{3} [\sqrt{2} + .88137] - R^4 \cdot \frac{4}{3}$$

$$F = 1.53039 \ R^3 - 1.333 \ R^4$$

This result is valid for $R \leq \frac{1}{\sqrt{2}}$, for the distance to the fartherest corner of the square must not exceed one. Otherwise the welfare expression is no longer valid.

For $n = 3$ one obtains

$$F = R^3 \cdot \frac{1}{2} \cdot \left[\frac{\sin \frac{\pi}{3}}{\cos^2 \frac{\pi}{3}} + \ln \tan (\frac{\pi}{4} + \frac{\pi}{6}) \right]$$

$$- R^4 \frac{1}{4} \cdot \left[\frac{\sin \frac{\pi}{3}}{\cos^3 \frac{\pi}{3}} + 2 \tan \frac{\pi}{3} \right]$$

$$= R^3 \frac{1}{2} \left[2\sqrt{3} + \ln \tan \frac{5\pi}{12} \right] - \frac{R^4}{4} [4\sqrt{3} + 2 \cdot \sqrt{3}]$$

$$= 2.390 \cdot R^3 - 2.598 \ R^4$$

Here $R \leq \frac{1}{2}$

for the distance from the center to the corner of the triangle is 2R, and the consumers' surplus is defined only for $r \leq 1$.

$$\frac{W}{A} = \frac{1}{\frac{1}{2}\tan\frac{\pi}{n}R^2} \int\limits_{o}^{\frac{\pi}{n}} \int\limits^{\frac{R}{m\varphi}} (1-r)r\ dr\ d\varphi - \frac{F}{2nR^2\tan\frac{\pi}{n}\cdot\frac{1}{2}}$$

$$= \frac{1}{\frac{1}{2}\tan\frac{\pi}{n}R^2} \int \frac{R^2}{2\cos^2\varphi} - \frac{R^3}{3\cos^3\varphi}\ d\varphi - \frac{F}{2\ n\ R^2} = \frac{1}{2}A_2 - \frac{R}{3}A_3 - \frac{F}{2\ n\ R^2}$$

$$0 = -\frac{1}{3}\int\frac{d\varphi}{\cos^3\varphi} + \frac{F}{n\ R^3} = -\frac{a_3}{3} + \frac{F}{n\ R^3}$$

$$R = \sqrt[3]{\frac{3F}{n\ a_3}}$$

$$\frac{W}{A} = \frac{2}{\tan\frac{\pi}{n}} \cdot [\ \frac{1}{2}a_2\ \ \frac{1}{3}a_3\ R] - \frac{F}{n\ \tan\frac{\pi}{n}\cdot R^2}$$

$$0 = -\frac{2}{3}a_3 + \frac{2\ F}{n\ R^3}$$

$$R = \sqrt[3]{\frac{3\ F}{n\ a_3}}$$

$$\frac{W}{A} = 1 - \frac{2}{3}\frac{1}{\tan\frac{\pi}{n}}\cdot a_3\ \sqrt[3]{\frac{3\ F}{n\ a_3}} - \frac{F}{\tan\frac{\pi}{n}\ n\ (\frac{3}{n}\frac{F}{a_3})^{\frac{2}{3}}}$$

$$= 1 - \frac{3}{\tan\frac{\pi}{n}}\cdot(\frac{a_3}{3})^{\frac{2}{3}}\ (\frac{F}{n})^{\frac{1}{3}}$$

$$= 1 - \frac{1}{\tan\frac{\pi}{n}}\cdot a_3^{\frac{2}{3}}\ (\frac{3}{n}\ F)^{\frac{1}{3}}$$

The achieved welfare per area is then

$$1 - 1.032 \sqrt[3]{F} \qquad \text{for triangles}$$

$$1 - 0.996 \sqrt[3]{F} \qquad \text{for squares}$$

$$1 - 0.9866 \sqrt[3]{F} \qquad \text{for hexagons}$$

$$1 - 0.984745 \sqrt[3]{F} \qquad \text{for circles.}$$

this ranking agrees with intuition.

4. Hotelling's Migration Model: The Steady State.

Economic inequalities are forever subject to forces of erosion. In two-dimensional space these take the particular form of diffusion. In the words of Hotelling "A ... tendency to spread out, to go from places of greater to places of less density appears in various phenomena connected with human society ... Human beings themselves show a marked tendency to spread out" (Hotelling p. 1225).

Similarly capital stock seeks niches unoccupied by other capital stock. Can spatial structures survive the onslaught of the forces of diffusion, and how? That is the concern of this chapter. We will begin with a brief summary of the Hotelling model of migration, that is fundamental to an analysis of spatial diffusion.

4.1 Pure diffusion: Homogeneous equation of Fick.

As a first step in the construction of a model of population growth and migration, one considers a pure model of migration based on diffusion only. Let $P(x,t)$ denote population density , i.e. population per unit area and let $\varphi(x,t)$ be the vector of migration whose direction is that of the flow of migrants and whose length is equal to the rate of flow through a unit cross section per unit of time.

If density is the driving force behind migration then

$$\varphi = -k \; grad \; P \tag{1}$$

or

$$\varphi = -kvP$$

The minus sign indicates that migration is in the direction of decreasing density. The diffusion constant k can be made equal to unity by a suitable choice of the time unit.

Next the thinning out of local population is equal to the thickening of the flow, i.e. its divergence. This is the law of conservation of matter

$$\frac{\partial P}{\partial t} = -\text{div } \varphi = -\frac{\partial \varphi_1}{\partial x_1} - \frac{\partial \varphi_2}{\partial x_2} \tag{2}$$

Combining (1) and (2)

$$\frac{\partial P}{\partial t} = \text{div grad } P$$

$$\frac{\partial P}{\partial t} = \nabla^2 P = \frac{\partial^2 P}{\partial x_1^2} + \frac{\partial^2 P}{\partial x_2^2} \tag{3}$$

This is known as Fick's law. It applies to heat, electricity and particles. We must add suitable boundary conditions. In a closed region, for instance, net migration across the boundary is zero. This means

$$\varphi_n = 0$$

on ∂A, or, using (1),

$$(\text{grad } P)_n = 0. \tag{4}$$

If one considers instead a one-dimensional region the equations are modified as follows. Let f denote flow to the right. Then

$$f = -\frac{\partial P}{\partial x} \tag{1a}$$

$$\frac{\partial P}{\partial t} = -\frac{\partial f}{\partial x} \tag{2a}$$

Hence

$$\frac{\partial P}{\partial t} = \frac{\partial^2 P}{\partial x^2} \tag{3a}$$

and

$$\frac{\partial P}{\partial x} = 0 \tag{4a}$$

at boundary points x_0, x_1.

It is also possible to consider an unbounded region with no boundary conditions or a region bounded on only one side.

The solution of Fick's equation depends also on initial conditions. The simplest case is that where all population P_o is initially concentrated at the origin. The solution of (3) for an unbounded region is then given by

$$P(x,t) = \frac{P_o}{4\pi t} \, e^{-\frac{x_1^2 + x_2^2}{4t}} \tag{5}$$

in the two-dimensional case and

$$P(x,t) = \frac{P_o}{2\sqrt{\pi t}} \, e^{-\frac{x^2}{4t}} \tag{6}$$

in the one-dimensional case. (cf. fig.4.1) For arbitrary initial conditions solutions are obtained from (5) or (6) by superposition.

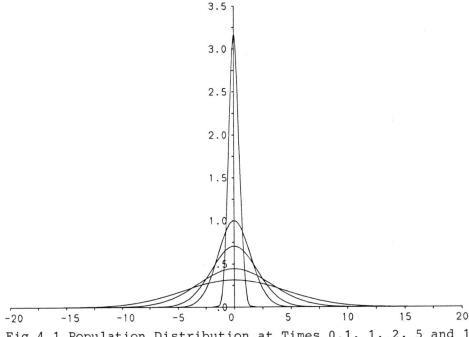

Fig.4.1 Population Distribution at Times 0.1, 1, 2, 5 and 10

Finite boundaries of an absorbing type (emigration) cause no change, but those of a reflecting type, i.e. a closed region will require modifications of this solution.

In a diffusion of type (5) or (6) the population maximum migrates outward. It is located at a point x where, in the one-dimensional case,

$$0 = \frac{\partial}{\partial t} \left(\frac{e^{-\frac{x^2}{4t}}}{\sqrt{t}} \right)$$

$$= \frac{1}{2} \frac{e^{-\frac{x^2}{4t}}}{t^{\frac{3}{2}}} + \frac{x^2}{4t^2} \frac{e^{-\frac{x^2}{4t}}}{t^{\frac{3}{2}}})$$

or

$$t = \frac{x^2}{2} .$$

(a fact noted also by Hotelling p.1232, equation (32)).

This means that the distance reached by the population maximum is proportional to the square root of time

$$x = \sqrt{2t} \tag{7}$$

In the two dimensional case for radially symmetric solution one has instead

$$r = \sqrt{2t}$$

where

$$r^2 = x_1^2 + x_2^2 .$$

In an unbounded region, the initial population P_o is eventually distributed at a uniform density of zero. In a closed bounded region it attains a positive uniform density.

4.2 Population Growth Added

When the diffusion model is to be applied to human migration, the facts of population growth and/or decline through birth and death must be added. This means that the thinning or growth of local populations depends not only on migration as expressed by v^2P but on local births and deaths as well. The classical way to describe these growth processes is by means of the logistic growth formula

$$g(P) = \gamma P \cdot (\sigma - P) \tag{7}$$

Here γ is the growth rate in the absence of physical restraints, and σ represents these physical restraints, i.e. the physically possible maximum population that can be sustained at any given location. (These concepts are taken from biology). Standardizing* both population and time units this becomes

$$g(P) = P(1 - P) \tag{8}$$

Entering this growth term into Fick's equation yields <u>Hotelling's equation of population growth and diffusion</u>

$$\frac{\partial P}{\partial t} = v^2P + P(1 - P) \tag{9}$$

Hotellings differential equation was rediscovered independently by J.G. Skellam, a well-known mathematical biologist (1951), who was apparently unaware of Hotellings' much earlier work. Skellam is considered the founder of an entire school of biologists studying animal and plant migration. For a recent survey cf. Okubo (1980).

---

*Actually we have used up one unit in standardizing to make the diffusion coefficient k = 1. Strictly speaking Hotelling's equation should still contain a diffusion coefficient k
$$\frac{\partial P}{\partial t} = kv^2P + P(1 - P) \tag{10}$$
We shall stay, however, with the simplified equation (9).

4.3 Steady State

Unlike Hotelling who wanted to explain westward migration in the United States as a historical process we will focus on a steady state, representing a system of order arising from the dynamics of production and migration. At first we leave out production and concentrate on the relationship between population and migration as perceived by Hotelling.

In a steady state

$$\frac{\partial P}{\partial t} = 0$$

and Hotelling's equation becomes

$$\nabla^2 P = P^2 - P \tag{1}$$

We will study this equation for two versions of homogeneous space
- the one-dimensional line

$$\frac{d^2 P}{dx^2} = P^2 - P \tag{2}$$

- the two-dimensional plane with a center at point zero. Let r be the distance from this center. The radially symmetric solutions of Hotellings equation must then satisfy

$$\frac{d^2 P}{dr^2} + \frac{1}{r} \frac{dP}{dr} = P(1 - P). \tag{3}$$

Hotelling himself considered linearized versions of his equation
- for small population levels

$$\nabla^2 P = \gamma P$$

- for large population levels closed to unity

$$\nabla^2 P = \delta(1 - P)$$

By a variable transformation

$$Q = 1 - P$$

and standardization the last equation can be transformed to

$$\nabla^2 Q = -\delta Q$$

so that both cases are contained in

$$\nabla^2 P = \mu P \qquad\qquad \mu = \pm 1$$

The linearized equation has been studied intensively by theoretical physicists (Carslaw, 1906). In particular the radially symmetric case is solved by Bessel functions.

When the flow of migrants is parallel, i.e. in one direction, the two-dimensional analysis may be replaced by a one-dimensional one.

4.4 Location of maxima and minima

Since in the Hotelling model the flow of migrants is in the direction of decreasing population density, the location of a minimum is necessarily at the endpoint of a flow line. This must be a boundary point and have positive outflow.

Maxima can occur both in the interior and on the boundary. In the interior the gradient must vanish. We have a singularity. This singularity is in the nature of a source since flows move away from it. On the boundary the gradient vanishes (no inflow) or is directed to the interior: a positive inflow. An outflow at a maximum is impossible.

In the one-dimensional case a symmetric solution of the equation exists provided there is an interior maximum, say at zero. For then

$$P(x) = P(-x)$$

implies

$$\frac{dP(x)}{dx} = -\frac{dP(-x)}{dx}$$

$$\frac{d^2P(x)}{dx^2} = \frac{d^2P(-x)}{dx^2}$$

so that to a right hand branch of a solution with

$$P'(0) = 0 \qquad \frac{dP}{dx} < 0 \qquad x > 0$$

there corresponds a left hand branch symmetric to the first with

$$\frac{dP}{dx} > 0 \qquad x < 0.$$

It is therefore sufficient to study the right hand branch. It implies zero flow at $x = 0$, i.e. a closure of the region at the origin. Solutions with positive inflow are found by placing the boundary point to the right of the mid point of the symmetric case.

The boundary condition $P'(0) = 0$ is therefore of special interest. It will be assumed throughout the rest of this chapter. It is also the type of boundary that was studied by biologists. The zero point is fixed as the center of a "habitat".

4.5 General Remarks

The admissible P values are restricted to

$$0 \leq P \leq 1$$

This implies that any solution to (1) or (2) is concave, and strictly concave for $0 < P < 1$.
From now on let $P = 0$ and $P - 1$ be excluded.

In the neighbourhood of a singular point

$$\text{grad } P = 0$$

or

$$\frac{dP}{dx} = 0$$

the solution must be decreasing. A singular point must be a maximum.

Let P_0 be the value of this maximum. Now at any point x in the neighbourhood

$$P'(x) = P'(0) + xP''(\theta x) = P''(\theta x)$$

If $P_0 > \frac{1}{2}$ then

$$P''(\theta x) = P(\theta x) [P(\theta x) - 1] < P(0) [P(0) - 1]$$

Hence for $x > 0$

$$P'(x) = x P''(\theta x)$$

$$\leq x P_0 [P_0 - 1] < 0$$

We have found a line of negative slope through a point $(x, P(x))$. The concave function $P(\Psi)$ must lie below this line for all $\Psi \geq x$. Hence $P(x)$ is positive only in a finite interval.

When $P(0) < \frac{1}{2}$ the same argument may be applied with

$$P''(\theta x) \leq P(x) [P(x) - 1] < 0.$$

4.6 Steady State Solution of the One-Dimensional Case

$$\frac{d^2P}{dx^2} = P^2 - P \qquad\qquad 0 \leq P \leq 1 \qquad\qquad (1)$$

A standard procedure for solving a second order differential equation of this type is as follows (cf. KAMKE, p.113)
Multiply (1) by $\frac{dP}{dx}$ and integrate

$$\int \frac{dP}{dx} \frac{d^2P}{dx^2}\, dx = \frac{1}{2} \int (\frac{dP}{dx})^2\, dx = \int (P^2 - P)\, \frac{dP}{dx} = \int (P^2 - P)dP$$

or

$$(\frac{dP}{dx})^2 = \frac{2}{3} P^3 - P^2 + a \qquad\qquad (2)$$

where a is a constant of integration. It must be large enough to render the right hand side of (2) non-negative since the left hand side is a square.

A case of prime interest to biologists (Skellam, 1951; Okubo, 1980) is that where population is distributed symmetrically around $x = 0$ and reaches zero at a finite distance $\frac{L}{2}$, so that the habitat has size L. Let P_o be the population level at the center. Then $\left[\frac{dP}{dx} \right]_o = 0$

$$0 = (\frac{dP}{dx})_o^2 = \frac{2}{3} P_o^3 - P_o^2 + a$$

yielding

$$a = P_o^2 - \frac{2}{3} P_o^3 > 0 \qquad\qquad (3)$$

for $0 < P_o < \frac{3}{2}$

(However, population levels above $P > 1$ are not considered; they are unstable).

In the first order equation (1) the variables may be separated and the solution obtained by quadrature

$$\int_{P_o}^{P} \frac{dp}{\pm \sqrt{a - p^2 + \dfrac{2p^3}{3}}} = \int_0^x dx = x$$

or since $P < P_o$

$$\int_{P}^{P_o} \frac{dp}{\sqrt{a - p^2 + \dfrac{2}{3} p^3}} = \pm x \tag{4}$$

Equation (4) determines x as a function of P. Its inverse exists where the right hand side of (2) is strictly positive. The habitat radius $\frac{L}{2}$ is then, using (3)

$$\int_0^{P_o} \frac{dp}{\sqrt{P_o^2 - \dfrac{2}{3} P_o^3 - p^2 + \dfrac{2}{3} p^3}} = \frac{L}{2} \tag{5}$$

For instance when $P_o = \dfrac{1}{2}$

$$\frac{L}{2} = \int_0^{\frac{1}{2}} \frac{dp}{\sqrt{\dfrac{1}{2} p - \dfrac{2}{3} p^3}}$$

$$L = 4.647$$

A solution to (4) with $P_o = \dfrac{1}{2}$ has been graphed in figures 4.2.

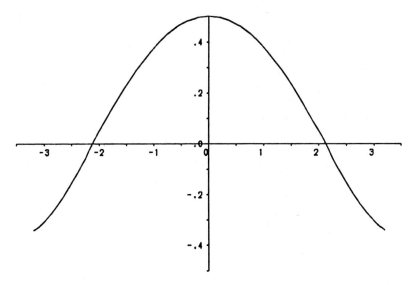

Fig.4.2 Symmetric Solution to Hotelling's Equation

The integral in (4) may be rendered more transparent by substituting

$$p = P_o - u$$

which yields

$$\int_0^{P_o-P} \frac{du}{\sqrt{2(P_o - P_o)^2 u + (2P_o - 1)u^2 - \frac{2}{3} u^3}} = x \qquad (6)$$

When $P_o = \frac{1}{2}$ this simplifies to

$$\sqrt{2} \int_0^{\frac{1}{2} - P} \frac{du}{\sqrt{u - \frac{4}{3} u^3}} = x \qquad (6a)$$

Although this is a fairly simple expression, no solution in closed form is known to exist.

Since the Hotelling model implies positive population growth at all levels $0 < P < 1$, there must be a positive outflow from any finite region as noted before. In fact the rate of outflow is given by

$$\varphi_n = -(\text{grad } P)_n$$

in the two-dimensional case

or

$$f = -\frac{dP}{dx}\Big|_{P=0} = -\frac{dP}{dx}\Big|_{x=\frac{L}{2}} \tag{7}$$

in the one-dimensional case at each end point of the habitat. Using (2)

$$f = \sqrt{a} = \sqrt{P_o^2 - \frac{2}{3} P_o^3} \tag{8}$$

From

$$\frac{df}{dP_o} \sim P_o - P_o^2 > 0$$

we conclude that outflow increases with the central (maximal) population level P_o.

The choice $P_o = 1$ yields as stationary solution the trivial one

$$P(x) \equiv 1. \tag{9}$$

Of course one can consider asymmetric situations. In general there will be a zero or positive inflow at one endpoint where population is at its maximum and a positive outflow at the other endpoint where population is at its minimum.

4.7   Perturbation Analysis

The periodic solutions can be approximated by the perturbation method. For formal reasons we pretend that the non-linearity in the Hotelling model is small. We deal with the case in one spatial dimension, and study the homogeneous solutions. The model is normalized by choosing time and population units that make diffusivity and saturation population unitary. Thus we study:

$$\frac{\partial^2 p}{\partial x^2} + p = p^2 , \tag{1}$$

but rewrite thus:

$$\ddot{p} + p = \epsilon p^2 , \tag{2}$$

To save space and make the formulas simpler we adopt the provisional convention that the dots denote partial spatial derivatives. The ϵ we know to be unitary, but we pretend it to be small. We are looking for a solution in the form of a series:

$$p(\xi) = p_0(\xi) + \epsilon p_1(\xi) + \epsilon^2 p_2(\xi) + \dots , \tag{3}$$

where:

$$\xi = (1 + \epsilon \kappa_1 + \epsilon^2 \kappa_2 + \dots)x . \tag{4}$$

The initial condition can without loss of generality be assumed to be:

$$p(0) = \alpha_0 + \epsilon \alpha_1 + \epsilon^2 \alpha_2 + \dots , \tag{5}$$

and:

$$\dot{p}(0) = 0 . \tag{6}$$

Substituting the attempted solution and equating the expressions assembled for equal powers of ϵ to zero separately we get the following sequence of equations:

$$\ddot{P}_o + P_o = 0 \ , \tag{7}$$

$$\ddot{P}_1 + P_1 = P_o^2 - 2\kappa_1\ddot{P}_o \ , \tag{8}$$

$$\ddot{P}_2 + P_2 = 2P_oP_1 - (\kappa_1^2 + 2\kappa_2)\ddot{P}_o - 2\kappa_1\ddot{P}_1 \ . \tag{9}$$

and so on in increasing complexity.

Equation (7) has the obvious solution:

$$P_o = \alpha_o\cos(\xi) \ . \tag{10}$$

as the sine component vanishes due to the initial conditions, the first derivative being zero. As was said this is no limitation as the whole periodic solution curve can be translated in space and still remain a solution. We can thus choose the origin at a local maximum for the solution curve.

Next, we can proceed to (8), which upon substitution of (10) becomes:

$$\ddot{P}_1 + P_1 = \frac{\alpha_o^2}{2} + \frac{\alpha_o^2}{2}\cos(2\xi) + 2\kappa_1\alpha_o\cos(\xi) \ , \tag{11}$$

where we have expanded the square of the cosine function into a constant and a cosine of the double frequency. This procedure will be followed with all the powers of the cosine function, expanding them in simple cosines of the basic period and its natural harmonics. We now notice that the last term in the right hand side of (11) would give rise to a so called secular term leading to a nonperiodic solution. We therefore have to make its contribution zero if we want a periodic solution. This we can do provided we put:

$$\kappa_1 = 0 \ . \tag{12}$$

Thus the equation is simplified and at the same time we gain the information that in the current approximation the period is not affected. Equation (11) is now readily solved by inspection and, in view of the initial condition, yields:

$$P_1 = \frac{\alpha_o^2}{2} - \frac{\alpha_o^2}{3} \cos(\xi) - \frac{\alpha_o^2}{6} \cos(2\xi) \ . \tag{13}$$

We carry out one more step in this series of approximations and just state the end result:

$$P_2 = -\frac{\alpha_o^3}{3} + \frac{29\alpha_o^3}{136} \cos(\xi) + \frac{\alpha_o^3}{9} \cos(2\xi) + \frac{\alpha_o^3}{48} \cos(3\xi) \ . \tag{14}$$

The following procedure is basically the same, but increases in computational complexity. By the elimination of secular terms we also get a new approximation of the period:

$$\kappa_2 = \frac{5}{12} \alpha_o^2 \ . \tag{15}$$

The period is thus increased, and we see that in general the period increases with the amplitude of the spatial wave.

To get the approximate solution we just add (10), (13), and (14) together, the smallness parameter being unitary. The procedure nevertheless converges pretty fast, and yields a good agreement with the simulated solutions. Unlike the power series solutions attempted the approximation is equally good everywhere in space.

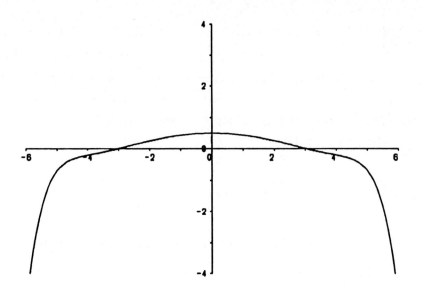

Fig.4.3 Power Series Solution

4.8 Solution of the Radially Symmetric Case by Taylor Series

In polar coordinates, the Laplace operator becomes (Courant–Hilbert, 1962, vol.II, p.242)

$$\Delta P = \frac{1}{r} \left[\frac{\partial}{\partial r} \left(r \frac{\partial P}{\partial r} \right) + \frac{\partial}{\partial \theta} \left(\frac{1}{r} \frac{\partial P}{\partial \theta} \right) \right]$$

Radial symmetry means $\frac{\partial}{\partial \theta} = 0$, hence

$$\nabla^2 P = \frac{d^2 P}{dr^2} + \frac{1}{r} \frac{dP}{dr}$$

and Hotelling's differential equation becomes

$$\frac{d^2 P}{dr^2} + \frac{1}{r} \frac{dP}{dr} = P^2 - P \tag{1}$$

One method of solution is to fit a Taylor series

$$P(r) = \sum_{n=0}^{\infty} a_n r^n \tag{2}$$

Substituting (2) in (1) yields

$$[(n + 2)(n + 1) + (n + 2)] \, a_{n+2} = -a_n + \sum_{i=0}^{n} a_i \, a_{n-i}$$

or

$$a_{n+2} = \frac{1}{(n+2)^2} \cdot \left(-a_n + \sum_{i=0}^{n} a_i \, a_{n-i} \right) \tag{3}$$

Differentiability at $r = 0$ in two-dimensional space requires

$$\frac{dP}{dr} \Big|_{o} = a_1 = 0$$

In fact

$$a_{2m+1} = 0 \qquad \text{for all m; the function is even.}$$

Moreover

$$a_2 = \frac{1}{4} (a_o^2 - a_o)$$

$$a_4 = \frac{1}{16} (- a_2 + 2a_o \, a_2)$$

The series turns out to be particularly simple when $P(0) = \frac{1}{2}$

For then
$$a_o = \frac{1}{2}$$

$$a_2 = - \frac{1}{16}$$

$$a_6 = \frac{1}{9216}$$

$$a_{10} = \frac{-1}{7372800}$$

and all coefficients $a_n = 0$ für $n > 2$, $n \neq 2 + 4m$.

This solution has been graphed in figure 4.3. It shows that the first root

$$P(r) = 0$$

is attained at

$$r = 2.85$$

which is the solution of the approximate equation

$$\frac{1}{2} - \frac{1}{16} r^2 + \frac{1}{9216} r^4 = 0$$

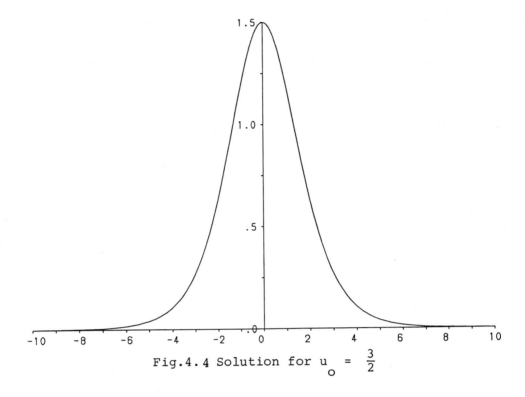

Fig.4.4 Solution for $u_o = \frac{3}{2}$

In the Hotelling model population migrates from points of higher density to points of lower density. In reality this applies on a large
scale. But in a smaller scale migration does take place from low density rural areas to higher density urban places. To explain this phenomenon a different mechanism must be assumed.

Also, the Hotelling model is not behavioral. The movement of people is
not modelled as the result of rational decisions but is interpreted me-
chanistically using the laws of motion found to apply to heat, to particles, and to electric charges. To integrate the Hotelling model into
economic theory, recourse must be had to concepts of utility. Moreover
utility itself must be considered the result of production processes
which in turn require modelling. Even a simple economic model is pref-
erable to a purely mechanistic one.

4.9 Alternative Interpretation of the Hotelling Model

It is desirable to give a behavioral interpretation of the Hotelling equation. One possibility is a follows.

a) migration φ is in the direction of and in strength equal to the gradient of "utility", the standard of living (say).

$$\varphi = \text{grad } u \tag{1}$$

b) utility equals per capita income

$$u = \frac{z}{P} \tag{2}$$

c) the production function is quadratic in terms of labour

$$z = P(1 - P) \tag{3}$$

hence

$$u = \frac{z}{P} = 1 - P$$
$$P = 1 - u \tag{4}$$

d) population growth is proportional to population and to the negative of utility

$$g = P \cdot (- u) =$$
$$= - (1 - u)u = u^2 - u \tag{5}$$

But in equilibrium population growth must equal net outflow

$$g = \text{div } \varphi \tag{6}$$
$$= \text{div } \varphi \text{ grad } u$$
$$= \nabla^2 u$$

Thus finally

$$v^2u = u^2 - u \tag{7}$$

This equation in terms of utility rather than population is mathematically identical with Hotellings equation for population.

A more satisfactory approach uses standard production functions such as Cobb Douglas and a more general linear relationship between population growth and utility, permitting both local population increases and decreases. This is done in the following chapter. In the next section we sketch an approach that leaves the mathematical form of the Hotelling Equation unchanged except for the sign of the right hand side.

4.10 Utility Model

Assumptions a) and b) of the previous section remain unchanged.
c') the production function is Cobb Douglas in terms of labour only.
    It has increasing returns to scale

$$z = bP^\beta \qquad\qquad \beta > 1 \tag{1}$$

d') population growth is proportional to population stock and is a
    linear decreasing function of per capita income

$$g = P(a - \alpha u) \tag{2}$$

Combining assumptions b) and c)

$$u = \frac{z}{P} = bP^{\beta-1}$$

$$P = \left(\frac{u}{b}\right)^{\frac{1}{\beta-1}} \tag{3}$$

Substituting (3) in (2)

$$g = \left(\frac{u}{b}\right)^{\frac{1}{\beta-1}} (a - \alpha u)$$

In a steady state

$$g = \operatorname{div} \varphi = \operatorname{div} \operatorname{grad} u = \Delta u \tag{4}$$

Thus

$$\Delta u = u^{\frac{1}{\beta-1}} (a\, b^{\frac{1}{1-\beta}} - \alpha\, b^{\frac{1}{1-\beta}} u)$$

Standardizing coefficients this becomes

$$\Delta u = u^m (1 - u) \tag{5}$$

where

$$m = \frac{1}{\beta - 1}$$

We shall examine two cases of particular interest:

$$\beta = 2 \qquad \text{yielding} \qquad m = 1$$
$$\beta = \frac{3}{2} \qquad \text{yielding} \qquad m = 2$$

The corresponding differential equations are

$$\nabla^2 u = u(1 - u) \tag{6}$$

and

$$\nabla^2 u = u^3 (1 - u). \tag{7}$$

The first is Hotelling's equation with reversed sign. It turns out that this sign change makes a major difference to the solution.

4.11 Solution for $u_o = \frac{3}{2}$

Proceeding as before we consider the one-dimensional case and multiply (6) by $\frac{du}{dx}$

$$\frac{d^2u}{dx^2} \frac{du}{dx} = \frac{1}{2} \frac{d}{dx} \left(\frac{du}{dx}\right)^2 = (u - u^2) \frac{du}{dx}$$

Integrating from zero to x

$$\frac{1}{2} \left(\frac{du}{dx}\right)^2 - \frac{1}{2} \left(\frac{du}{dx}\right)_o^2 = \frac{u^2}{2} - \frac{u^3}{3} \qquad (8)$$

Once more we focus on symmetric solutions of (6). This requires

$$\frac{du}{dx}\Big|_o = 0.$$

Hence

$$\frac{du}{dx} = \pm \sqrt{u^2 - \frac{2u^3}{3}}$$

or

$$\frac{du}{dx} = \pm \sqrt{\frac{2}{3}} \cdot u \sqrt{\frac{3}{2} - u}$$

The + sign for positive x implies migration away from the center. We consider first the more interesting case of migration to the center

$$u(0) > u(x) \qquad x \neq 0$$

$$\sqrt{\frac{3}{2}} \int_u^{u(0)} \frac{du}{u\sqrt{\frac{3}{2} - u}} = x \qquad\qquad x \geq 0$$

To obtain a closed form solution let

$$u = v^2 \qquad\qquad du = 2vdu$$

yielding

$$\int_{v}^{v(0)} \frac{dv}{v\sqrt{\frac{3}{2} - v^2}} = \frac{x}{\sqrt{6}}$$

This is solved by (Selby, p.420)

$$-\frac{1}{\sqrt{\frac{3}{2}}} \ln \left[\frac{\sqrt{\frac{3}{2}} + \sqrt{\frac{3}{2} - v^2}}{v} \right] \Bigg|_{v}^{v(0)} = \frac{x}{\sqrt{6}}$$

or

$$\frac{\sqrt{\frac{3}{2}} + \sqrt{\frac{3}{2} - v^2}}{v} = e^{c - \frac{x}{2}}$$

where c is a constant of integration

$$(ve^{c - \frac{x}{2}} - \sqrt{\frac{3}{2}})^2 = \frac{3}{2} - v^2$$

$$v = \frac{\sqrt{3}}{2} \cdot \frac{2}{e^{c - \frac{x}{2}} + e^{-c + \frac{x}{2}}}$$

$$u(x) = \frac{3}{2} \cdot \frac{1}{\cos^2(\frac{x}{2} - c)}$$

But $u(0) = \frac{3}{2}$ requires $c = 0$, i.e. symmetry implies $c = 0$. Thus finally

$$u(x) = \frac{3}{2} \operatorname{sech}^2 (\frac{x}{2}) \qquad\qquad\qquad (9)$$

where

$$\text{sech}(y) = \frac{2}{e^u + e^{-u}}$$

is the hyprobolic secant. (Figure 4.4)

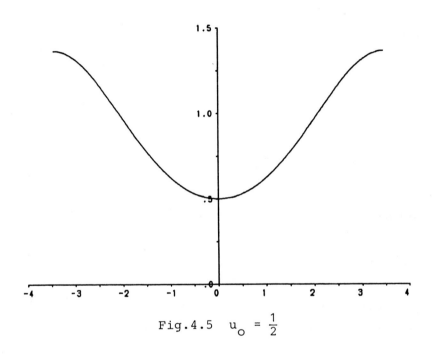

Fig.4.5 $\quad u_o = \frac{1}{2}$

Expression (9) is the only symmetric solution to the one-dimensional equation (6) that is defined for the entire line. As shown by (6) it is concave for small x (when u > 1) and convex for large x. It approaches u = 0 as x goes to infinity.

Economically speaking this solution describes migration to the center from either side either in an infinite region with no immigration or a finite region of size L with immigration. The rate of immigration at each side is then

$$f = -\frac{du}{dx}\Big|_{\frac{L}{2}} = \frac{2}{3} \cdot \frac{\sin h \frac{L}{4}}{\cos^2 h \frac{L}{4}}$$

$$= \frac{4}{3} \frac{e^{\frac{1}{4}} - e^{-\frac{L}{4}}}{(e^{\frac{L}{4}} + e^{\frac{L}{4}})^2} \tag{10}$$

For example, when the habitat boundary is located at $P = \frac{1}{2}$, $\frac{L}{2}$ is determined by

$$\frac{1}{2} = \frac{3}{2} \sec h^2(\frac{L}{4})$$

$$\sqrt{3} = \frac{e^{\frac{L}{4}} + e^{-\frac{L}{4}}}{2}$$

from which

$$\frac{L}{2} = 2.2924$$

The total population in the habitat may now be calculated as follows.
Since $\beta = 2$, $P = u$, the total population P is

$$P = 2 \int_0^\infty P \, dx = 2 \int_0^\infty u(x)dx = 2 \int \frac{3}{2} \frac{4}{(e^{\frac{x}{2}} + e^{-\frac{x}{2}})^2} \, dx$$

$$= 12 \int_0^\infty \frac{e^x}{(1 + e^x)^2} \, dx$$

Let $\quad e^x = y \qquad\qquad x = \ln y \qquad\qquad d = \frac{dy}{y}$

$$P = 12 \int_0^\infty \frac{dy}{(1 + y)^2} = -12 \frac{1}{1 + y} \Big|_0^\infty = 12$$

4.12 General Solution by Quadrature

When $u(0) \neq \frac{3}{2}$ the symmetry condition

$$\frac{du}{dx}\Big|_o = 0$$

requires that in equation (8)

$$\frac{1}{2}\left(\frac{du}{dx}\right)_o^2 = \frac{u_o^2}{2} - \frac{u_o^3}{3} + \frac{a}{2} = 0 \tag{11}$$

with a suitable constant of integration $\frac{a}{2}$. Clearly

$$a = \frac{2}{3}u_o^3 - u_o^2$$

The first order equation becomes

$$\frac{du}{dx} = \pm \sqrt{u^2 - \frac{2u^3}{3} + a}$$

It may be solved by quadrature along the lines of section 4.6 as in the original Hotelling Model. Sample solutions are graphed in figures 4.5 and 4.6.

The nature of the (symmetric) solutions depends critically on u_o, the utility level at the center. We summarize:

$u_o = 0$ then $u(x) \equiv 0$. No flow.

$0 < u_o < 1$ $u(x)$ is initially increasing and convex, turning increasing and concave where $u(x) = 1$. It rises to a maximum where $\frac{du}{dx} = 0$, and this constitutes a natural boundary point with zero closs flow (Fig.4.5).

$u_o = 1$ $(x) \equiv 1$. No flow.

$1 < u_o < \dfrac{3}{2}$

u(x) is initially concave and decreasing.
At u(x) = 1 lies a turning point, beyond
which u(x) is convex and declining.
$\dfrac{du}{dx} = 0$ occurs for positive u at a finite
distance x, constituting a boundary point
with zero cross flow (Fig.4.6).

$u_o = \dfrac{3}{2}$

$u(x) = \dfrac{3}{2} \operatorname{sech}^2(\dfrac{x}{2})$. (Fig.4.7)

$u_o > \dfrac{3}{2}$

u(x) is decreasing, initially concave,
turning convex at u(x) = 1.
Positive inflow is required at the u = 0
boundary point. When u is negative it
is also concave. No periodicity.
(Fig.4.8)

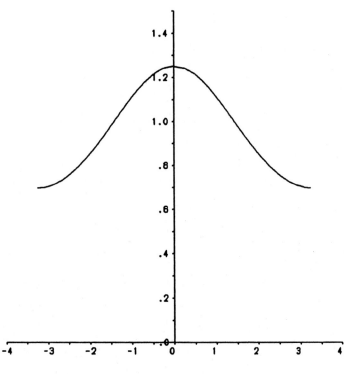

Fig.4.6 $u_o = \dfrac{5}{4}$

4.13 Case $\beta = \frac{3}{2}$

A less extreme case of increasing returns, compared to $\beta = 2$ is $\beta = \frac{3}{2}$. In that case we obtain equation (7). Its one-dimensional version is

$$\frac{d^2u}{dx^2} = u^2(1 - u)$$

As before this may be integrated to yield

$$\frac{1}{2}\left(\frac{du}{dx}\right)^2 = \frac{u^3}{3} - \frac{u^4}{4} + a$$

A symmetrical solution requires that this expression vanishes for $u = u_0$. In particular $a = 0$ if and only if $u_0 = \frac{4}{3}$.

Separating variables we have then

$$\frac{du}{-\sqrt{\frac{2}{3}u^3 - \frac{1}{2}u^4}} = dx$$

$$dx = \frac{du}{u^{\frac{3}{2}}\sqrt{\frac{2}{3} - \frac{1}{2}u}} = \frac{\sqrt{2}\,du}{u^{\frac{3}{2}}\sqrt{\frac{4}{3} - u}}$$

Set $u = y^2$ $du = 2y\,dy$. Then

$$x = \int_0^x dx = 2\sqrt{2} \int_{\sqrt{u}}^{\sqrt{u_0}} \frac{dy}{y^2\sqrt{\frac{4}{3} - y^2}}$$

$$x = -2\sqrt{2}\; \frac{\sqrt{\frac{4}{3} - y^2}}{\frac{4}{3}y} \Bigg|_{\sqrt{u}}^{\sqrt{u_0}}$$

$$\frac{\sqrt{2}}{3} x = \frac{\sqrt{\frac{4}{3} - u}}{\sqrt{u}} - \frac{\sqrt{\frac{4}{3} - u_o}}{u_o}.$$

From $u_o = \frac{4}{3}$

$$\frac{2}{9} x^2 = \frac{\frac{4}{3} - u}{u}$$

$$u = \frac{12}{9 + 2x^2}$$

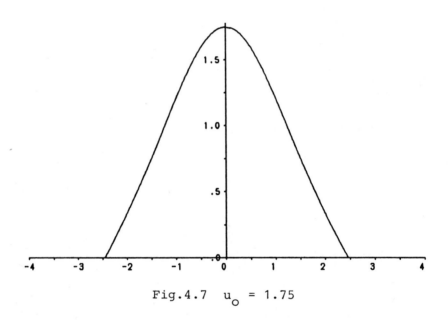

Fig.4.7 u_o = 1.75

This is the only symmetric solution defined over the entire line. As before solutions exist for bounded intervals provided $1 < u_o \leq \frac{4}{3}$.

The population in the habitat is then

$$p = 2 \int_o^\infty P\ dx = 2 \int_o^\infty u^2\ dx = 2 \cdot \left(\frac{12}{9}\right)^2 \int_o^\infty \frac{1}{(1 + \frac{2}{9} x^2)^2}$$

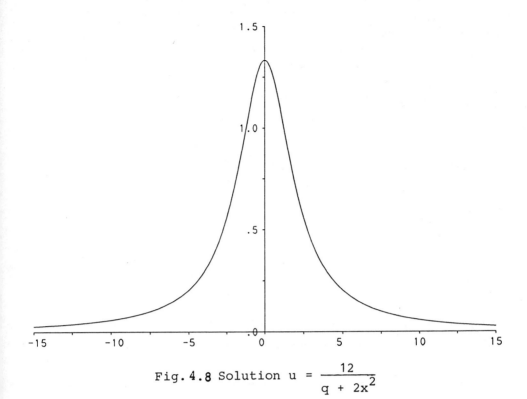

Fig. 4.8 Solution $u = \dfrac{12}{q + 2x^2}$

Let $u = \dfrac{\sqrt{2}}{3} x$ $dx = \dfrac{3}{\sqrt{2}} dy$

$$p = \frac{32}{9} \cdot \frac{3}{\sqrt{2}} \int_{0}^{\infty} \frac{1}{(1 + y^2)^2} \, dy$$

$$= \frac{16 \sqrt{2}}{3} \left[\frac{x}{2(1 + x^2)} + \frac{1}{2} \arctan x \right] \Big|_{0}^{\infty}$$

$$p = \frac{8 \sqrt{2}}{3} \cdot \frac{\pi}{2} = \frac{4 \sqrt{2}\, \pi}{3} = 5.9238$$

4.14 Linearized Hotelling Equation: 1 Dimension

Hotelling himself has suggested replacing the quadratic right hand side by linear approximation suitable to the two limiting cases

  • very small population $g(P) - \gamma P$ $\gamma > 0$
  • population close to the maximum of unity $g(P) = 1 - \mu P$

We shall consider instead that the rate of population growth is a step function of the type

$$g(P) = mP$$

with

$$m = \begin{cases} 1 & P < \dfrac{1}{2} \\[2mm] 0 & P = \dfrac{1}{2} \\[2mm] -1 & P > \dfrac{1}{2} \end{cases}$$

It is straight forward to go from there to the more general case

$$m = \begin{cases} \gamma & P < \bar{P} \\[2mm] 0 & P = \bar{P} \\[2mm] -\mu & P > \bar{P} \end{cases}$$

We are thus led to the differential equation

$$\frac{\partial P}{\partial t} = \frac{\partial^2 P}{\partial x^2} + mP$$

In the manner of mathematical physics we consider solutions in which the effects of time and space are separated

$$P(x,t) = Q(x) \cdot F(t)$$

$$Q \frac{\partial F}{\partial t} = F \frac{\partial^2 Q}{\partial x^2} + m F Q$$

$$\frac{1}{F} \frac{\partial F}{\partial t} = \frac{1}{Q} \frac{\partial^2 Q}{\partial x^2} + m$$

Since the left hand does not depend on x and the right hand does not depend on t both must be constant, say λ. Then

$$\frac{\partial F}{\partial t} = \lambda F \tag{1}$$

$$\frac{\partial^2 Q}{\partial x^2} = (\lambda + m)Q \tag{2}$$

Consider once more solutions symmetric to the origin which vanish at given boundary points $\pm \frac{L}{2}$.

$$Q(\tfrac{L}{2}) = Q(-\tfrac{L}{2}) = 0$$

This requires that $\lambda + m \leq 0$ and leads to

$$Q(x) = \cos \left(\sqrt{|\lambda + m|}\, x + a \right)$$

$$\sqrt{|\lambda + m|} \cdot \frac{L}{2} + a = \frac{\pi}{2} + 2\pi n$$

which is solved by

$$a = 0$$

and

$$\sqrt{-(\lambda + m)} = \frac{\pi}{L}(1 + 4n)$$

or

$$\lambda_n = -m - \frac{\pi^2}{L^2}(1 + 4n)^2$$

The general solution is then

$$P(x,t) = \sum_{n=1}^{\infty} A_n \, e^{\lambda_n t} \, \cos\,(x\sqrt{-\lambda_n - m})$$

(The boundary condition requires that $A_o = 0$.).

When $m > 0$ all non zero solutions are damped and disappear as time goes on. When $m < 0$

$$\lambda_1 = -m - 25\frac{\pi^2}{L^2}$$

Suppose that

$$m = -\left(\frac{5\pi}{L}\right)^2$$

so that

$$\lambda_1 = 0$$

Then a stationary solution exists

$$P(x) = A_1 \, \cos\,\frac{5\pi}{L}\,x$$

$m < 0$ means positive population growth. There is emigration at both boundary points at the rate

$$A_1 \frac{5\pi}{L} \sin \frac{\pi}{2} = \frac{A_1 5\pi}{L}$$

4.15 Radially Symmetric Case

The Hotelling equation is

$$\frac{\partial P}{\partial t} = \frac{\partial^2 P}{\partial r^2} + \frac{1}{r} \frac{\partial P}{\partial r} + mP$$

Separating into a time dependent and space dependent function

$$Q \frac{\partial F}{\partial t} = F \frac{\partial^2 Q}{\partial r^2} + F \frac{1}{r} \frac{\partial Q}{\partial r} + m F Q$$

$$\frac{1}{F} \frac{\partial F}{\partial t} = \frac{1}{Q} \frac{\partial^2 Q}{\partial r^2} + \frac{1}{rQ} \frac{\partial Q}{\partial r} + m = \lambda$$

yielding

$$\frac{\partial F}{\partial t} - \lambda F = 0$$

$$r^2 \frac{\partial^2 Q}{\partial r^2} + r \frac{\partial Q}{\partial r} + (m - \lambda)r^2 Q = 0$$

The last is Bessel's equation with $n = 0$ and eigenvalues $m - \lambda$.

We shall not discuss this any further since it does not lead into new territory.

4.16 Stability of the Hotelling Model

We want to consider the stability of stationary solutions to the Hotelling model:

$$\dot{p} = p(1 - p) + \nabla^2 p \ , \tag{1}$$

where the dot represents the partial time derivative, and the Laplacian operator the sum of the two direct second partial space derivatives. Suppose we have found a stationary solution:

$$\pi(1 - \pi) + \nabla^2 \pi = 0 \ . \tag{2}$$

We define a small deviation:

$$z(x_1, x_2, t) = p(x_1, x_2, t) - \pi(x_1, x_2) \tag{3}$$

from the stationary solution, and insert it into the first equation. Then, using the stationarity condition for π, and putting the small z squared equal to zero, we get:

$$\dot{z} = (1 - 2\pi)z + \nabla^2 z \ . \tag{4}$$

We next multiply this equation through by z and integrate over the region of space in consideration. Thus:

$$\frac{1}{2} \frac{\partial}{\partial t} \iint_R z^2 dx_1 dx_2 = \iint_R (1 - 2\pi)z^2 dx_1 dx_2 + \iint_R z\nabla^2 z dx_1 dx_2 \ . \tag{5}$$

According to Gauss's Integral Theorem, however,

$$\iint_R z\nabla^2 z dx_1 dx_2 + \iint_R (\nabla z)^2 dx_1 dx_2 = \oint_{\partial R} z\frac{dz}{dn} ds = 0 \ , \tag{6}$$

where the last curve integral on the boundary is zero whenever p satisfies the same boundary conditions as does π .

Collecting the results we have:

$$\frac{1}{2} \frac{\partial}{\partial t} \iint_R z^2 dx_1 dx_2 = \iint_R (1 - 2\pi) x^2 dx_1 dx_2 - \iint_R (\nabla z)^2 dx_1 dx_2 < 0, \quad (7)$$

provided that:

$$\pi < \frac{1}{2} \qquad\qquad (8)$$

everywhere.

Thus any stationary solution is locally asymptotically stable, provided the periodic solution nowhere deviates by more than $\frac{1}{2}$ of the spatially homogeneous solution at the saturation level, and provided the boundary conditions are not changed. As there is an infinity of such (spatially) periodic solutions with different period and amplitude (within the limits prescribed by stability), there are infinitely many such locally stable attractors, and we can expect all kinds of transitions whenever the deviations from such a stable stationary solution are large enough.

5. Migration Model with Production

5.1 Growth

One disadvantage of the original Hotelling (1921) model is that the
supply of means of subsistance is taken as a given constant, independent of time and of population (labour force). The model is indeed more
suitable in biology than in economics, as demonstrated by its sucess in
the former field after it was rediscovered by Skellam 30 years after
Hotelling.

Man, unlike other animals, produces his own means of subsistance, and
due to technological progress (labour division, and accumulation of
capital) this production has become more and more efficient over time.
(Even for biological populations food supply tends to vary over time,
but the variation tends to be cyclical rather than secular as indicated
by the Lotka-Volterra systems.) Finally, given the supply of means of
subsistance, there is no mechanical once and for all fixed relation between it and the "saturation population" at which the rate of change of
population is exactly zero. Attitudes as to what is an acceptable per
capita living standard are apt to change over time, and human societies
have a long experience in adjusting net reproduction to all but a given
ratio to population.

Therefore we suggest as in Puu (1985) to replace the growth term:
$\dot{p} = p(1 - p)$ by:

$$\dot{p} = p(1 + \alpha(\beta p^2 - p^3) - \gamma p) \, , \tag{1}$$

where we have introduced the simplest possible production function with
initially increasing and eventually decreasing returns to scale:

$$q = \alpha(\beta p^2 - p^3) \, . \tag{2}$$

It is the truncated Taylor series of any production function with variable returns to scale so as represented in the textbooks. The coefficient α measures technological efficiency, whereas β represents

production scale. Thus, the transition from increasing to decreasing returns occurs at $p = \frac{1}{2}\beta$, production is maximal at $p = \frac{2}{3}\beta$, and is reduced to zero at $p = \beta$. Occasionally this last decreasing section is defined away by the assumption of free disposal, but if we keep it we can let it represent increasing difficulties of getting rid of indus- trial wastes.

In both formulas we have chosen convenient measurement units of time and of population to make the growth rate and the stationary population (in the Hotelling model) unitary. It should be noted that we have kept this "natural" supply of means of subsistence (fruits, game, fish) that supported mankind at early stages of development.

The coefficient γ represents social attitudes to the acceptable per capita income that leads to stationarity.

We have given intuitive arguments concerning the realism of asumptions for the introduction of a production function with increasing–decreas- ing returns. There are, however, additional reasons for such a change, pertaining to the functioning of the whole model. As we saw before the solutions to the original Hotelling model are always periodic, but their minima dip in negative populations and thus the solutions make no economic sense.

Introducing a higher order of nonlinearity leads to a more stratified model with several intervals of alternating growth and decrease, and we may expect economically sensible spatial population patterns with al- ternating concentrations and rerefactions. The change of parameters may also be expected to cause loss of stability with resulting bifurca- tions.

Let us start by discussing the stationary solutions to the modified growth equation. They fulfil the condition:

$$p(1 + \alpha(\beta p^2 - p^3) - \gamma p) = 0 \ . \tag{3}$$

One solution is obvious, i.e., p = 0 . This solution is always unstable
as we will see later on. The number of nontrivial stationary solutions
depends on the discriminant of the remaining parenthesis where we rear-
range the terms and divide through by α:

$$p^3 - \beta p^2 + \frac{\gamma}{\alpha}p - \frac{1}{\alpha} = 0 . \tag{4}$$

Setting:

$$Q = \frac{\gamma}{3\alpha} - \frac{\beta}{9} , \tag{5}$$

and

$$R = \frac{1}{2\alpha} + \frac{\beta^3}{27} - \frac{\beta\gamma}{6\alpha} , \tag{6}$$

we obtain the discriminant:

$$D = Q^3 + R^2 \tag{7}$$

Substituting for Q and R we get:

$$108\alpha^3 D = 4\alpha^2\beta^3 - \alpha\beta^2\gamma^2 - 18\alpha\beta\gamma + 4\gamma^3 + 27\alpha . \tag{8}$$

If D < 0 there are three different nontrivial stationary roots, if
D > 0 there is only one. When D = 0 at least two roots are coincident.
When Q = R = 0 all three roots coincide. To see that the degenerate
cases by no means are unlikely we note that Q = 0 implies $\alpha\beta^2 = 3\gamma$, and
that R = 0 implies $\alpha\beta^3 = 27$. Setting $\alpha = 1$, $\beta = 3$, $\gamma = 3$, we get a triple root for p = 1. The parameters being positive and population being
in the range where the production function makes sense the case is possible. From this triple point all possible cases can be produced by
minute parameter changes. For instance the constellation $\alpha = 1.2$,
$\beta = 3$, $\gamma = 3.4$ will be used in illustrating the case of three roots
p = 1, $1 \pm 1/\sqrt{6}$, of course in addition to the trivial zero root.

To consider the stability of the dynamical system suppose we have a root $p = \pi$, such that the stationarity condition:

$$\pi(1 + \alpha(\beta\pi^2 - \pi^3) - \gamma\pi) = 0 \qquad (9)$$

is fulfilled.

Define the small deviation from equilibrium:

$$z = p(t) - \pi . \qquad (10)$$

Substituting this in the growth euqation (1) we obtain after deleting all powers of z which is small and using the stationarity condition (9):

$$\dot{z} = (1 + \alpha(3\beta\pi^2 - 4\pi^3) - 2\gamma\pi)z . \qquad (11)$$

As the coefficient of z is independent of it the system is linear. The stability of π depends on the sign of:

$$\mu = 1 + \alpha(3\beta\pi^2 - 4\pi^3) - 2\gamma\pi . \qquad (12)$$

We immediately see that the zero solution $\pi = 0$ is unstable as then $\mu = 1 > 0$. The borderline between stability and instability occurs when $\mu = 0$. Putting μ in (12) equal to zero and using the stationarity condition (9) to eliminate π we get:

$$4\alpha^2\beta^3 - \alpha\beta^2\gamma^2 - 18\alpha\beta\gamma + 4\gamma^3 + 27\alpha = 0 . \qquad (13)$$

which according to (8) implies $D = 0$. A zero discriminant, indicating the coincidence of several roots, is thus associated with the loss of stability of stationary solutions, i.e. with bifurcations.

5.2 Diffusion

Once we have introduced an explicit production function it is obvious
that we should also modify Hotelling's original diffusion term.
According to his own argument population diffuses away from more to
less densely populated areas because under diminishing returns per
capita production would be negatively related to population. Making
diffusion proportionate to the Laplacian of population, however, implies that this negative relation is a linear one. A linear approximation is reasonable as a first step in analyzing marginal change, but
the general flavour of Hotelling's logistic growth term is that of
global modelling and nonlinearities.

By consequence we should then use the explicit production function introduced to relate the flow of migrants to per capita output, rather
than to population density. We thus assume a net flow of migrants
$p\nabla(q/p)$ going in the direction of steepest increase of per capita production. Its force is proportionate to this maximum rate of spatial
living standard difference, and to the density of population, account-
ing for the number of potential migrants that may react to these differences. The source density of this flow is:

$$-\nabla \cdot (p\nabla \frac{q}{p}) \ . \tag{14}$$

where the sign is reversed as we deal with an attractive force rather
than with a repulsive one.

Skellam (1953) added a different argument for diffusion. Nonhuman populations do in general not act conciously to migrate to places they
know to be less crowded and hence more affluent with food. The same
diffusion effect, however, arises from purely stochastic movement in
space. If each animal in a certain time period takes a step in an arbitrary direction (moving like a Brownian particle), then there are more
animals moving out than in at a location of relative concentration,
whereas the reverse holds at a relative rarefaction. This movement
makes sense even in human populations due to change of location for
reasons of education, marriage and the like. Thus we add a random dif-

fusivity relating directly to the density of population, but introducing per capita production as an index of diffusivity. This is to ac-
count for an increased radius of movement due to better means of transportation as a component in an increasing living standard. This second
diffusion term thus reads:

$$\nabla^2(\tfrac{q}{p}\, p) \; . \tag{15}$$

Adding both diffusion terms (14) and (15) we get:

$$\nabla^2(\tfrac{q}{p}\, p) - \nabla \cdot (p\nabla \tfrac{q}{p}) = \nabla \cdot (\tfrac{q}{p}\, \nabla p) \; , \tag{16}$$

by an elementary identity from vector analysis.

5.3   Growth and Diffusion

We can now combine the modified growth and diffusion terms to get the
complete model:

$$\dot{p} = p(1 + q - \gamma p) + \nabla \cdot (\tfrac{q}{p}\, \nabla p) \; . \tag{17}$$

Generally, the diffusion term should be preceded by a multiplicative
constant but we again choose units of measurement (in this case for
distance in space) so as to make it unitary.

Substituting from (2) for q we get:

$$\dot{p} = p(1 + \alpha(\beta p^2 - p^3) - \gamma p) + \tfrac{1}{6}\nabla^2 \alpha(3\beta p^2 - 2p^3) \tag{18}$$

The next task is to investigate the stationary solutions and the stability of those.

5.4 Stationary Solutions in One Dimension

As in the case of the original Hotelling model it is easiest to deal with the one-dimensional case. The diffusion term then becomes:

$$\frac{\partial}{\partial x}(\frac{q}{p}\frac{\partial p}{\partial x}) \quad , \tag{19}$$

which after substitution for q from (2) becomes:

$$\frac{\partial}{\partial x}(\alpha(\beta p - p^2)\frac{\partial p}{\partial x}) \quad . \tag{20}$$

The condition for stationarity is then:

$$(p - \gamma p^2 + \alpha\beta p^3 - \alpha p^4) + \frac{\partial}{\partial x}(\alpha(\beta p - p^2)\frac{\partial p}{\partial x}) = 0 \quad . \tag{21}$$

Expressions like this usually yield a so called first "energy" integral. We obtain this by multiplying through by $\alpha(\beta p - p^2)\partial p/\partial x$ and integrating. In this way we get:

$$(\frac{\beta}{3}p^3 - \frac{1 + \beta\gamma}{4}p^4 + \frac{\gamma + \alpha\beta^2}{5}p^5 - \frac{\alpha\beta}{3}p^6 + \frac{\alpha}{7}p^7)$$

$$\frac{\alpha}{2}(\beta p - p^2)^2(\frac{\partial p}{\partial x})^2 = E \quad , \tag{22}$$

where E is a constant. The level curves for various values of E in the phase plane for p and its first (spatial) derivative are illustrated in Figure 5.1 for the case $\alpha = 1.2$, $\beta = 3$, $\gamma = 3.4$ with three different nontrivial roots to the growth term. We see that the solutions are periodic. There are two disjoint sets of closed orbits separated by a saddle which corresponds to the unstable case of a homogeneous unitary population.

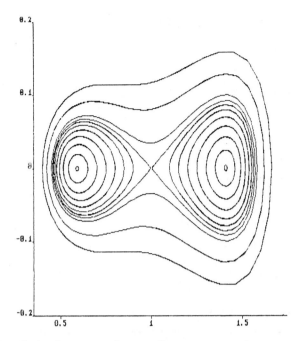

Fig.5.1 Constant "energy" curves in phase space.

These results correspond well to the results of simulation, illustrated in Figure 5.2, showing invariably periodic solutions. Unlike the case for the original Hotelling model they never extend into the region of negative population. We also see that the (spatial) period increases with the amplitude.

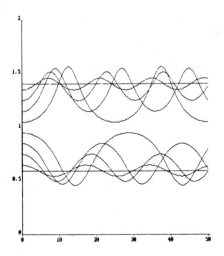

Fig.5.2 Stationary solution curves over space.

5.5 Stability

To investigate the stability of the model

$$\dot{p} = p(1 + \alpha(\beta p^2 - p^3) - \gamma p) + \frac{1}{6} \nabla^2 \alpha(3\beta p^2 - 2p^3) \tag{23}$$

is a little more tricky than in the case of the original Hotelling model. Suppose we have a stationary solution $p = \pi$ that makes the right hand side of equation (23) identically zero at all locations. It can be a homogeneous one, or it can be periodic over space so as indicated above. We define

$$z(x_1, x_2, t) = p(x_1, x_2, t) - \pi(x_1, x_2) \tag{24}$$

as a small deviation from equilibrium and introduce it into the dynamic equation (23). As the expression becomes a little complex, let us deal with the growth term and the diffusion term separately.

By substitution the growth term becomes:

$$\pi(1 + \alpha(\beta\pi^2 - \pi^3) - \gamma\pi) + (1 + \alpha(3\beta\pi^2 - 4\pi^3) - 2\gamma)z , \tag{25}$$

where we have deleted all powers of z, which is assumed small. We note that the first term of (25) is the growth term of (23) with the stationary solution substituted and hence identically equals the negative of the diffusion term for the stationary solution:

$$- \frac{1}{6} \nabla^2 \alpha(3\beta\pi^2 - 2\pi^3) . \tag{26}$$

Adding the diffusion and growth terms with the last substitution we note that, the Laplacian operator being linear, we can assemble the terms preceded by ∇^2, so that:

$$\dot{z} = (1 + \alpha(3\beta\pi^2 - 4\pi^3) - 2\gamma\pi)z$$
$$+ \frac{1}{6} \nabla^2 \alpha(3\beta(\pi + z)^2 - 3\beta\pi^2 - 2(\pi + z)^3 + 2\pi^3) . \tag{27}$$

At this stage we note that the first term on the right is linear in z, and that its coefficient depends on π solely, being in fact the formal linearization of the growth term.

$$w(\pi,z) = 6\alpha\pi(\beta - \pi)z + 3\alpha(\beta - 2\pi)z^2 - 2z^3 \ . \tag{28}$$

The growth equation (27) for z then becomes:

$$\dot{z} = (1 + \alpha(3\beta\pi^2 - 4\pi^3) - 2\gamma\pi)z + \frac{1}{6}\nabla^2 w \ . \tag{29}$$

To proceed we multiply this equation through by w , again cancelling all powers of z. In this way we get:

$$6\alpha(\beta\pi - \pi^2)z\dot{z} = 6\alpha(\beta\pi - \pi^2)(1 - \alpha(3\beta\pi^2 - 4\pi^3) - 2\gamma\pi)z^2$$
$$+ \frac{1}{6}w\nabla^2 w \ . \tag{30}$$

Integrating over space we get:

$$\frac{\partial}{\partial t} \iint 3\alpha(\beta - \pi)z^2 dx_1 dx_2 = \iint 6\alpha(\beta\pi - \pi^2)(1 - \alpha(3\beta\pi^2 - 4\pi^3)$$
$$- 2\gamma\pi)z^2 dx_1 dx_2 - \frac{1}{6} \iint (\nabla w)^2 dx_1 dx_2 \ , \tag{31}$$

where the last term follows from the Gauss integral theorem when w is zero on the boundary. We see that w is in fact zero whenever z is, which must hold on the boundary whenever p and π fulfil the same boundary conditions.

Thus, the diffusion term leads to damping. As $\pi < \beta$ whenever production is positive, stability depends entirely on the sign of the expression (12):

$$\mu = 1 + \alpha(3\beta\pi^2 - 4\pi^3) - 2\gamma\pi \ , \tag{32}$$

stated again for convenience.

If the sign is negative on the whole region then the stationary solution investigated is stable. This is a sufficient condition.

For the case $\alpha = 1$, $\beta = 3$, $\gamma = 3.4$ used as illustration in the one dimensional case the intervals $[0.21, 0.78]$ and $[1.25, \infty)$ for π lead to stability. Accordingly, both the homogeneous solutions 0.59 and 1.41, as well as the ondulating ones in figures 5.1 – 5.2 with limited amplitude are stable. The stability condition is not satisfied for the large orbits outside the saddle loop in Figure 5.1.

6. Catastrophe Theory Applied to the Refraction

of Traffic

One of the main issues of these contributions concerns how macroscopic
structure – like market areas, agglomerations, and the like – arise
though no spatial inhomogeneities are present. Resources are assumed to
be mobile, generally there are no local productivity differences assumed, and transportation flows do not necessarily conform to any pre-
assigned radial patterns.

In the chapter related to von Thünen, we saw how saddle points arouse
in a nonlinear transportation model, these points representing locations of particularly intensive transportation.
It is also possible to find such unexpected concentrations of traffic
starting from a different point of departure in classical location
analysis. the refraction law for traffic, passing two media like land
and water, discovered by Palander (1935) and von Stackelberg (1938)
establishes a parallel between the behaviour of light rays in optics
and transportation routes. The phenomenon of light caustics (by reflec-
tion or refraction) observed in a cup of coffee should therefore also
turn up when traffic crosses a curved coastline. What corresponds to
the highly illuminated caustic would be a curve at infinite traffic
intensity.

The case is easy to study by analytical means if the coastline is assumed to be a circular arc and the routes are broken straight lines (as
they are under the Palander–Stackelberg assumption of constant but different transportation costs on land and on sea.) Catastrophe theory,
however, certifies that the qualitative results hold for any shape of
the coastline and for any generalized transportation model of the type
suggested in Beckmann (1952, 1953). Concerning the formal analysis of
caustics we refer to Saunders (1980).

To make things precise suppose we deal with a semicircular costline of
unit radius. Suppose, moreover, that transportation cost is unitary on

sea and is k > 1 on land. (Transportation cost is thus uniform and isotropic in each medium, so that routes are straight lines, possibly broken at the coastline). Finally, suppose, that the points interior to
the coastline communicate with an infinitely distant point to the
right. Putting the origin in the centre of the circle, and denoting the
euclidean coordinates by x, y we see that all the routes at sea are
parallel to the x-axis. As mentioned we can remove the restrictive assumptions one by one, but they facilitate modelling and agree with the
formulation in classical spatial economics. the case is illustrated in
fig.6.1.

Let us denote a point on the boundary by cos α, sin α and an interior
point by x, y. The distance between them is
$\sqrt{(\cos \alpha - x)^2 + (\sin \alpha - y)^2}$ and we get transportation cost on land by
multiplying the distance with the cost rate k. As for transportation
on sea we only need to consider the part that is different for different points of the coastline. Normalizing it to zero at the rightmost
point ($\alpha = 0$) the distance, and cost, on sea is $1 - \cos \alpha$. Accordingly,
transportation cost from the point x, y through the boundary point, in
direction α from the origin, is

$$V = k \sqrt{(\cos \alpha - x)^2 + (\sin \alpha - y)^2} + 1 - \cos \alpha \qquad (1)$$

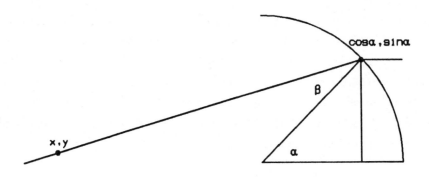

Fig.6.1. The symbol conventions illustrated

The direction α can be chosen so as to minimize V, and this yields the condition

$$\frac{dV}{d\alpha} = k \frac{x \sin \alpha - y \cos \alpha}{\sqrt{(\cos \alpha - x)^2 + (\sin \alpha - y)^2}} + \sin \alpha = 0 \ . \tag{2}$$

To see that this corresponds to the Palander-Stackelberg law of refraction we can proceed as follows. Define the unit vectors

$$A = (\cos \alpha, \ \sin \alpha)$$

and

$$B = \frac{(\cos \alpha - x, \ \sin \alpha - y)}{\sqrt{(\cos \alpha - x)^2 + (\sin \alpha - y)^2}}$$

Obviously the vector product of these equals

$$\frac{y \cos \alpha - x \sin \alpha}{\sqrt{(\cos \alpha - x)^2 + (\sin \alpha - y)^2}} = \sin \beta$$

where β is the angle between the two unit vectors. However, β is also the angle of refraction as shown in Fig.6.1. On substituting from the last equation into (2) we obtain

$$k = \frac{\sin \alpha}{\sin \beta} \tag{3}$$

As α is the angle of incidence, (3) is nothing but the Palander-Stackelberg law. Figure 6.2. illustrates how the pencil of parallel transportation routes is refracted at the circular boundary and how they, in fact, form a caustic. For increased visibility the rays are not extended after they cross the horizon, but in reality they, of course, continue and are scattered again in all directions. If we differentiate (2) once more with respect to α and put the second derivate equal to zero we obtain the following condition for tangency between the set of confluent lines and their apparent envelope

$$k^2(x \sin \alpha - y \cos \alpha)(x \cos \alpha + y \sin \alpha)$$

$$= \cos \alpha \sin \alpha \, ((\cos \alpha - x)^2 + (\sin \alpha - y)^2) + \sin^2\alpha \, (x \sin \alpha - y \cos \alpha)$$

In principle the last equation could be used along with equation (2) to eliminate α obtaining an implicit relation between x and y, but this is computationally not so easy. Instead we can eliminate x, and y in turn to obtain the envelope by x and y given as functions of the parameter α

$$x = \cos \alpha \, (1 - \frac{\sin^2\alpha}{k^2})(\cos \alpha + \frac{(k^2 - \sin^2\alpha)^{1/2} + \cos \alpha}{k^2 - 1}) \tag{4}$$

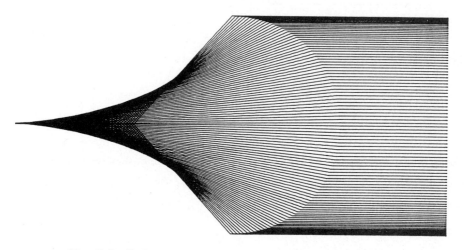

Fig.6.2. Refraction by a semicircular coastline.

and
$$y = \sin^3 \alpha / k^2 \tag{5}$$

valid for $|\alpha| \leq \frac{1}{2}\pi$.

A set of such curves for various values of k is illustrated in Fig.6.3. where the caustics become more and more concentrated to the neighbourhood of the origin as k gets higher and higher.

We can now relate the story to catastrophe theory. The envelopes or caustics are the bifurcation sets in control space (x, y). The state

variable, subject to choice under the cost minimization assumption, is
α. The three-dimensional space α as a function of x and y is a typical
surface related to the cusp catastrophe. It would not be easy to solve
α explicitly from (2), but we can benefit from our knowledge that we
deal with a ruled surface formed by lifting each traffic ray to the

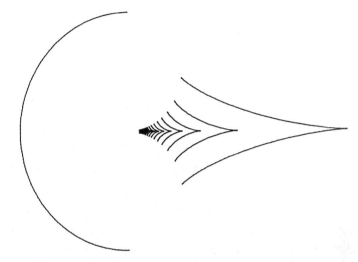

Fig.6.3. The caustics for various k.

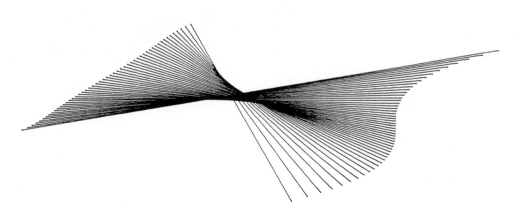

Fig.6.4. Catastrophe surface

level α. It is then easy to make a computer graph of the whole surface.
It is illustrated in fig.6.4.

The Palander-Stackelberg model was generalized by Beckmann (1) to a case where transportation cost could vary continuously over space. The optimal flows of traffic then became general vector fields obeying certain optimality conditions equivalent to Huygens' Principle. Denoting the vector field by $\phi = (\phi_1(x, y), \phi_2(x, y))$ and its euclidean norm by $|\phi| = (\phi_1^2 + \phi_2^2)^{1/2}$ the optimality condition reads

$$k(x, y)\phi/|\phi| = \text{grad } \lambda \tag{6}$$

where λ is a potential function that can be interpreted as total transportation cost along a route. For (6) any kind of vector field can arise on sea and on land, but the law of refraction still holds on any boundary where there is sudden discontinuity of transportation rates. Accordingly the formation of caustics still occurs in qualitatively the same manner as in the simplified example, as catastrophy theory ascertains that the phenomena we have treated are universal. They hold for any irregular flow field, and the exact shape of the convex boundary need not be specified.

7. The Weberian Location Triangle

Moses (1958) places the location problem firmly in the setting of production theory and concludes that the problem of location must be
solved in connection with the choice of operation scale and technology.
Only if the technology is of the Leontief type with fixed coefficients
and has constant returns to scale can the location decision be dissociated from the production decision.

However, Moses is so interested in what happens in commodity space that
the corresponding manifestations of his analysis in geographical space
are left implicit. To bring these out is the modest purpose of the following digression. To that end two popular production functions, the
Cobb-Douglas and the CES, are used, and the isoprofit curves in geographical space are depicted. These curves generalize the Weberian
isodapans, coinciding with the latter whenever the technology is of
Leontief type.

We can thus directly see how much substitution and scale adjustment af-
fects the choice of location. In fact almost all points along the broken line joining the Weber point with the locations of input sources
become equivalent with a unitary elasticity of substitution, and with
higher elasticities the Weber point is definitely dominated by the input source locations.

So, the firm will "locate at the source of one of the inputs" as Moses
states not only when the inputs can be substituted "in the extreme"
(i.e. with straight isoquants), but with much more moderate elasticities of substitution. Moses fails to see this because he does not investigate the "iso-outlay curves" more closely. Otherwise he would have
found that they could have touched the isoquants in more than one
point.

This multimodality naturally introduces the possibility of bifurcations
of both the hard and the soft types.

Suppose for definiteness that we deal with a location problem where the Weberian triangle is equilateral with side $\sqrt{3}$ and choose a coordinate system where $(1,0)$ is the location of the market and $(-1/2, \sqrt{3}/2)$, $(-1/2, -\sqrt{3}/2)$ are the locations of input supplies. Moreover, assume that all three transportation rates are unitary, so that with a Leontief production function the origin becomes the Weber point. Around this profit maximum we could draw the set of isodapans.

The distances that output and inputs must be transported to a location (x,y) then are:

$$s = \sqrt{(x-1)^2 + y^2} \tag{1}$$

$$s_1 = \sqrt{(x + \tfrac{1}{2})^2 + (y - \tfrac{\sqrt{3}}{2})^2} \tag{2}$$

and

$$s_2 = \sqrt{(x + \tfrac{1}{2})^2 + (y + \tfrac{\sqrt{3}}{2})^2} \tag{3}$$

Let the f.o.b. prices accordingly be $(p - s)$, $(p_1 + s_1)$, $(p_2 + s_2)$. These prices enter the ratios equated to the marginal productivities.

With production functions of the Cobb-Douglas and CES types it is an elementary exercise to calculate the marginal productivities, equate them to the price ratios, then solve for inputs and output and calculate profits.

Assuming a slightly decreasing returns to scale (0.8) the Cobb-Douglas function is:

$$q = (v_1 v_2)^{0.4} \tag{4}$$

and a CES function with elasticity of substitution 2 is.

$$q = (\sqrt{v_1} + \sqrt{v_2})^{1.6} \tag{5}$$

The corresponding profit functions are:

$$\Pi = (\frac{p - s}{5})^5 \, (\frac{4}{(p_1 + s_1)(p_2 + s_2)})^2 \tag{6}$$

and

$$\Pi = (\frac{p - s}{5})^5 \, (\frac{4}{p_1 + s_1} + \frac{4}{p_2 + s_2})^4 \tag{7}$$

respectively.

In Figures 7.1 and 7.2 we illustrate the isoprofit curves for levels 75 percent to 95 percent of the Weberian "optimum". It can be noted that in the CES case there are additional disjoint sets of curves around the input locations representing profit levels of 110 to 150 percent of the Weberian reference value. It is obvious that in this case the Weber point is dominated by two much sharper local maxima at the locations of input supply.

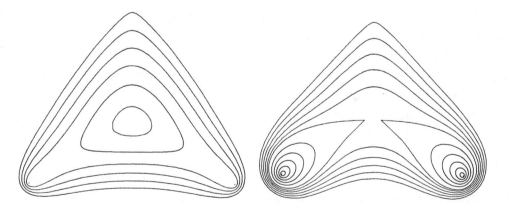

Fig.7.1 Isoprofit curves for   Fig.7.2 Isoprofit curves for
         Cobb-Douglas function.   CES function.

It is also interesting that in the Cobb-Douglas case, where the Weber point is indisputably best, almost the whole location triangle is covered by the 90 percent isoprofit curve.

To complete the picture we illustrate the profit surfaces for the two cases in Figures 7.3 and 7.4.

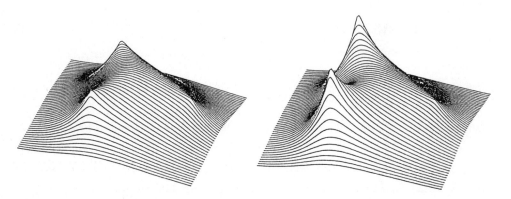

Fig.7.3 Profit surface for   Fig.7.4 Profit surface for
         Cobb-Douglas function.   CES function.

In the CES case the input location peaks dominate the picture. As the pictures have been drawn for equal input prices, the peaks have equal height. The outcome is bimodal, and hence unstable. Any infinitesimal change of input prices causes a jump in location.

We conclude the discussion by showing the shape of the isoprofit curves for some considerably lower elasticities of substitution (0.5 and 0.1 respectively) in Figures 7.5 and 7.6. The last ones, as expected, look like text-book isodapans.

Our basic conclusion is that any reasonable substitution possibilities reduce the profits from optimal Weberian location to very tiny amounts. The substantial profits from location choice can be obtained when location at the input sources is best, and then we can expect bifurcations to occur when prices change.

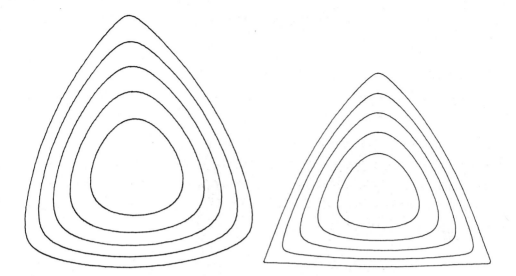

Fig.7.5 Isoprofit curves. Elasticity of substitution = 0.5

Fig.7.6 Isoprofit curves.Elastic-
ity of substitution = 0.1

8. Order from Disorder

8.1 Resource Location and Population Location

Suppose that a resource (oil, ore, coal, fertile land, water) is available at a given density $q(x_1, x_2)$. The resource may be transported at a given cost k or else it is immobile but its product may be so transported. The labor requirements for this transformation activity are small and may be neglected. Also the labor input into transportation is assumed to have no immediate effect on the distribution of population.

Per capita consumption of the resource or its product is assumed to be constant, equal to one unit.

We seek to determine the optimum locational distribution of a mobile population.

Since consumption of goods is fixed, welfare depends only on the consumption of space. Let the utility function be logarithmic in terms of space available per capita

$$u = \ln\left(\frac{1}{p}\right) \tag{1}$$

where p = population density.
Aggregate utility is then an entropy

$$\iint -p \ln p \, dx_1 . dx_2$$

The welfare function to be maximized is this aggregate utility net of transportation costs for the commodity consumed

$$- \iint [p \ln p + k \, |\varphi|] dx_1 \, dx_2 \tag{2}$$

Here φ denotes the vector of commodity flow. We have the following constraints

$$\iint p \, dx_1 dx_2 = M \tag{3}$$

total population M must be settled. Then local excess demand equals
q - p and in equilibrium this equals the negative divergence of the
flow field

$$\nabla\varphi + q - p = 0 \tag{4}$$

(cf. Beckmann-Puu, 1985, pp.11-16)
Maximizing (2) subject to the constraints (3) and (4) is best achieved
by considering a Lagrangean

$$\iint -p \ln p - k \, |\varphi| + \lambda \, (\nabla\varphi + q - p) \, dx_1 \, dx_2 + \mu[M - \iint p \, dx_1 \, dx_2]$$

Differentiating with respect to p and setting this zero yields

$$- \ln p - 1 - \lambda - \mu = 0 \tag{5}$$

$$p(x) = a \, e^{-\lambda(x)} \tag{6}$$

where

$$a = e^{-1 - \mu} = \text{constant} \tag{7}$$

Variation with respect to φ yields (cf. Beckmann-Puu 1985, p.34)

$$k \, \frac{\varphi}{|\varphi|} = \nabla\lambda \tag{8}$$

Here $\lambda = \lambda(x)$ represents the price of the resource or commodity.

Equation (6) suggests that inaccessible locations, i.e. those with high
transportation costs for the commodity should be sparsely settled. In
particular when the resource is found at a single location,
say x = 0, then

$$\lambda(x) = kr \qquad (9)$$

where

$$r = \sqrt{x_1^2 + x_2^2} \qquad (10)$$

is the distance from the resource location. Then

$$p(r) = p(0) \, e^{-k \, r} \qquad (11)$$

Population density decreases exponentually from the center.

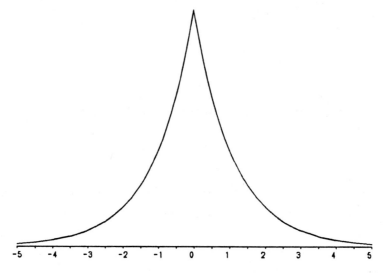

Fig.8.1 Exponential Density Profile

A standard version of this model is the monocentric city where the single resource represents both job and shopping opportunities, all concentrated in a single center.

The exponential decrease of density is compensation for the cost of transporting oneself (and familiy) to the center of the action. But the underlying idea is a more general one: a balancing of accessibility against spaciousness.

8.2 Continuous Distribution of Resources and the Aggregate Production Function

How are resources such as land utilized in a spatial economy when population expands? Diverging now from the standard model of a uniform plain assume that land differs with respect to its productivity s, measured as output of a standardized consumption good per unit of land and labor. At first we ignore transportation of the product and assume instead that all production is for local consumption only. Labor must be applied to land in fixed proportions: one unit of labor to one unit of land.

At low levels of population only the most productive land is utilized. Let land productivity vary between unity and infinity.

$$1 \leq s < \infty$$

and let the quality of land have a given distribution

$$m(s)ds$$

Observe that, with fixed coefficients land must have a certain minimum quality in order that a unit of labor can earn enough to feed itself and progeny.

Total available land is then

$$M = \int_1^\infty m(s)ds \; < \; \infty \tag{1}$$

Let x be the marginal quality of land used by a population L. If only land of productivity x and above is utilized then

$$L = \int_{x}^{\infty} m(s)ds \tag{2}$$

This determines the marginal quality of land as a function of the labor supply L.

Aggregate output is given by

$$Z = \int_{x}^{1} s\ m(s)ds \tag{3}$$

The aggregate production function

$$Z = Z(L) \tag{4}$$

is then determined by the distribution of land quality or its density m(s) .

As an illustrative example consider a Pareto distribution of land quality

$$m(s) = a\ s^{-\alpha} \qquad s \geq 1 \tag{5}$$

This distribution may also be considered as an approximation to a log normal distribution of land quality. It can be argued that land productivity is the result of many factors which act in a multiplicative fashion.

Now

$$L = a \int_{x}^{\infty} s^{-\alpha} = \frac{a}{1-\alpha} s^{-\alpha+1} \Big|_{x}^{\infty}$$

This expression is finite if and only if $\alpha > 1$
yielding

$$L = \frac{a}{\alpha-1} x^{1-\alpha} \tag{6}$$

Output is

$$Z = a \int_{x}^{\infty} s^{1-\alpha} ds = \frac{a}{2-\alpha} s^{2-\alpha} \Big|_{x}^{\infty}$$

Finiteness now requires the more stringent assumption

$$\alpha > 2$$

Then

$$Z = \frac{a}{\alpha - 1} x^{2-\alpha} \tag{7}$$

Combining (6) and (7)

$$Z = \frac{a}{\alpha - 2} (\frac{\alpha - 1}{a} L)^{\frac{\alpha - 2}{\alpha - 1}}$$

$$Z = b \, L^{\beta} \tag{8}$$

with

$$b = a^{\frac{1}{\alpha-1}} (\alpha - 1)^{\frac{\alpha-2}{\alpha-1}} (\alpha - 2)^{-1} \qquad\qquad \beta = \frac{\alpha-2}{\alpha-1}$$

This is a Cobb Douglas production function as first shown by H. Houthakker (1953). Since $0 < \alpha - 2 < \alpha - 1$ it shows decreasing returns to scale. These are due to the fact that soils of lesser and lesser quality must be put into production as population expands.

We obtain a cost function from (8) by solving for L

$$L = (\frac{Z}{b})^{\frac{1}{\beta}}$$

Identifying cost with labor input

$$C = cZ^{\gamma} \qquad\qquad \gamma > 1 \qquad\qquad (9)$$

Diminishing returns imply increasing unit costs.

Compare to this the aggregate production function that results in a homogeneous environment when transportation to the market is included in the picture. Let transportation require only labor as input. The labor requirement is proportional to the ton kilometers of material moved. Let the supply area of the von Thünens city have a radius R. Then

labor input into production $\qquad\qquad \pi R^2 \qquad\qquad$ (10)
(if one unit of labor is applied to one unit of land)

labor input into transportation $\qquad h \cdot \int_o^R r \cdot 2\pi r \; dr = h\frac{2\pi}{3} R^3$ (11)

output $\qquad\qquad\qquad\qquad\qquad b \cdot \pi R^2 \qquad\qquad$ (12)

It is convenient in this case to go straight to the cost function rather than derive it from a production function

$$C = \pi R^2 + h \; 2\frac{\pi}{3} R^3$$

$$C = \frac{1}{b} Z + \frac{2\pi h}{3} \left(\frac{Z}{b\pi}\right)^{\frac{3}{2}} \qquad\qquad (13)$$

using (12).
Equation (13) shows once more increasing unit costs. The production function is the inverse of equation (13). Both have been graphed in fig.8.2.

The picture becomes more transparent when local agriculture production is described by a linear homogeneous Cobb Douglas function. In terms of densities x(r) = labour input per unit are

z(r) = product output per unit area.   Thus

$$z(r) = bx^{\alpha}(r) \qquad\qquad b > 0 \qquad 0 < \alpha < 1 \qquad\qquad (14)$$

Let transportation be produced from labour only, one unit of transportation output from one unit of labour.

To obtain an aggregate production function for the combined agricultural and transportation sectors we calculate

$$Z = \int_o^R 2\pi r \; b \; x^{\alpha}(r) dr \qquad\qquad \text{agricultural output}$$

$$X = \int_o^R 2\pi r \; x(r) dr \qquad\qquad \begin{array}{l}\text{labour input into}\\ \text{agricultural production}\end{array}$$

$$T = \int_o^R 2\pi r^2 \; b \; x^{\alpha}(r) dr \qquad\qquad \begin{array}{l}\text{labour input into transportation}\\ \text{of agricultural products to the}\\ \text{center.}\end{array}$$

$$L = X + T \qquad\qquad \text{total labour input.}$$

To determine the optimal allocation of labour to agricultural production and transportation, maximize Z with respect to x(r) for a given
amount of total labour L. The result is

$$x(r) = \lambda(1 - \frac{r}{R})^{\frac{1}{1-\alpha}} \qquad\qquad\qquad (15)$$

where λ is a suitable constant (derived from a Lagrangean multipli-
er). This shows, how optimal land use requires a decreasing density of
labour input and by implication of product output with increasing distance from the center

$$z = b\lambda^{\alpha}\left(1 - \frac{r}{R}\right)^{\frac{\alpha}{1-\alpha}} \tag{16}$$

From this, finally, (Beckmann, 1988)

$$Z = B \cdot L^{\frac{2-\alpha}{3-2\alpha}} \tag{17}$$

Observe that the exponent is less than unity

$$0 < \frac{2 - \alpha}{3 - 2\alpha} < 1 \tag{18}$$

Constant returns to scale in local production still yield decreasing returns to scale in aggregate production. The reason is that increasing agricultural output incurs a convexly increasing amount of transportation costs.

Thus decreasing returns to scale in agriculture may be understood as a result of either the diminishing quality of soil put under cultivation or of increasing transportation costs.

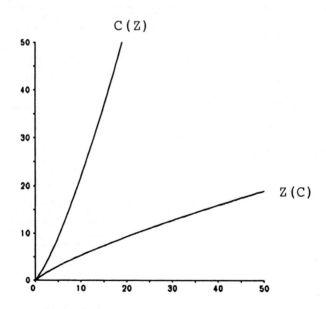

Fig.8.2 Cost and Production Function

Epilog

Imagine a world like von Thünen's plain of uniform fertility, but without a central city. Assume instead that alle production activities are
governed by constant returns to scale. There is then no need for any
city or any deviation from a uniform density of settlement. This world
is without spatial structure. Production of all goods is carried out
everywhere for local consumption. All things exhibit a uniform spatial
density. Each place is like any other place.

By contrast consider a world where resource endowment varies from place
to place and transportation costs are insurmountable. Once more production is for local consumption only; it may have decreasing or increasing returns to scale. The range of products offered will differ greatly
amoung locations according to what resources are available. If tech-
niques of production are not diffused, local traditions will enhance
the differences in availability and costs of local products.

Levels of welfare, standards of living, will vary according to the ratio of local population to local resources. Increasing returns to scale
will favour locations that, owing to fertile land and other resources,
are able to support population at a high density.

Quite another scenario is that of a world with zero transportation
costs. Production activities with increasing returns to scale at all
levels are now concentrated in one location only. This location is
arbitrary and different for different activities. Economies of joint
location (agglomeration) induce clustering as in the well-known example
of steel mills and rolling mills where heat can be saved by locating
together. Spatial variety is here the sole result of specialization and
concentration of production in order to reap economies of scale.
Resource transportation being free, their local availability does not
matter anymore.

When resources are distributed uniformly but transportation is not free, the result is a Central Place System.

Reality is like none of the three extremes nor is it exactly a Central Place System. Rather it is a combination of the three basic scenarios. As transportation costs have fallen and as technical progress has transformed constant returns activities into activities with increasing returns to scale, what differences now exist among locations have become differences of size and density of settlements, pushing into the background differences resulting from local resource availability. In that sense the world is becoming more uniform. The world economy has little use for local color. Even so spatial structures emerge and will continue to survive; as we have tried to show in this monograph.

References

Abraham,R.H. and Shaw, (1982-1985), C.D. Dynamics: The Geometry of
   Behavior.I-IV (Aerial Press, Santa Cruz).

Andronov,A., Pontryagin, L., (1937), Systemes grossiers, Computes
   Rendus de l'Academie des Sciences de l'URSS 14 247-250.

Arnold,V.I., (1983), Geometrical Methods in the Tehory of Ordinary
   Differential Equations (Springer, New York).

Beckmann,M.J., (1952), A continuous model of transportation,
   Econometrica 20, pp.643-660.

Beckmann,M.J.,(1953), The partial equilibrium of a continuous space
   market, Weltwirtschaftliches Archiv 71, pp.73-89.

Beckmann,M.J., (1971), Spatial Olygopoly Revisited: An Examination of
   some Strategies in Mill Pricing in one and two dimensional Markets,
   North East Regional Science Review 1, p.1-20.

Beckmann,M.J., (1975), Spatial Price Policy Revisited, The Bell Journal
   of Economics, p.619-630.

Beckmann,M.J., (1988), An Economic Model of Urban Growth, in: Cities
   and their Vital Systems, National Academy Press, Washington, D.C.

Beckmann,M.J. and Puu,T., (1985), Spatial Economics (North-Holland,
   Amsterdam).

Braudel,F., (1981), The Structures of Everyday Life, William Collins
   Sons & Co Ltd., Publishers, Inc.

Carslaw,H.S., (1906), Introduction to the Theory of Furios Theories and
   Integrals and the Mathematical Theory of the Conduction of Heat.
   London McMillan & Company.

Courant,R. and Hilbert,D., (1937), Methods of Mathematical Physics,
   New York: Interscience Publishers (german edition Springer-Verlag
   Berlin).

Frisch,R., (1965), Theory of Production, Reidel Publishing Company/
   Dordrecht-Holland.

Gilmore,R., (1981), Catastrophe Theory for Scientists and Engineers
   (Wiley, New York).

Hirsch,M.W., Smale, S., (1974), Differential Equations, Dynamical
   Systems and Linear Algebra (Academic Press, New York).

Hotelling,H., (1978), A Mathematical Theory of Migration, Environment and Planning, Vol.10 pp.1223-1239.

Houthakker, H.S., (1955), The Pareto distribution and the Cobb-Douglas production function in activity analysis. REStud 23:27 no.1.

Kamke,E., (1961), Differentialgleichungen, Lösungsmethoden und Lösungen I, Gewöhnliche Differentialgleichungen 7. Aufl., Akademische Verlagsgesellschaft Geest und Portig KG, Leipzig, p.113.

Lösch,A., (1954), The Economics of Location, New Haven, Yale University Press (German edition 1940).

Mills, E.S. and Lav, M.R., (1964), A Model of Market Areas with Free Entry, Journal of Political Economy, pp.278-88.

Okubo,A., (1980), Diffusion and Ecological Problems: Mathematical Models, Heidelberg, Springer-Verlag.

Palander,T.F., (1935), Beiträge zur Standortstheorie (Almqvist & Wiksell, Uppsala).

Peixoto,M.M., (1977), Generic properties of ordinary differential equations, MAA Stud.Math.14, pp.52-92.

Poston,T. and Stewart,I., (1978), Catastrophe Theory and its Applications (Pitman, London).

Puu,T., (1979), Regional modelling and structural stability, Environment and Planning A 11, pp.1431-1438.

Puu,T., (1982), Structurally stable transport flows and patterns of location, RR-82-84, International Institute of Applied Systems Analysis, Laxenburg, Austria.

Puu,T. and Weidlich,W., (1986), The stability of hexagonal tessellations, in: Space-Structure-Economy (Von Loeper Verlag, Karlsruhe).

Samuelson,P.A., (1947), Foundations of Economic Analysis (Harvard University Press, Harvard).

Samuelson,P.A., (1952), Spatial price equilibrium and linear programming, Amer.Econ.Rev.42, pp.283-303.

Saunders,P.T., (1980), An Introduction to Catastrophe Theory (Cambridge University Press, Cambridge).

Selby,S.M., (1969), Standard Mathematical Tables. Cleveland, Ohio: The Chemical Rubber Co., 17th ed.

Skellam,J.G., (1951), Random Dispersal in Theoretical Populations, Geometrika 38, pp.196-218.

von Stackelberg,H., (1938), Das Brechungsgesetz des Verkehrs, Jahr-
    bücher für Nationalökonomie und Statistik 148, p.680.
von Thünen,H., (1921), Der isolierte Staat. Waentig, Jena.
Toshiharu,M. and Ishikawa,T., (1988), The Shape of Market Areas and
    Welfare, unpublished manuscript.

NAME INDEX

SUBJECT INDEX